Series/Number 07-085

PROCESSING
DATA
The Survey Example

LINDA B. BOURQUE
University of California, Los Angeles

VIRGINIA A. CLARK
University of California, Los Angeles

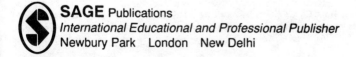

SAGE Publications
International Educational and Professional Publisher
Newbury Park   London   New Delhi

For information address:

 SAGE Publications, Inc.
2455 Teller Road
Newbury Park, California 91320
E-mail: order@sagepub.com

SAGE Publications Ltd.
6 Bonhill Street
London EC2A 4PU
United Kingdom

SAGE Publications India Pvt. Ltd.
M-32 Market
Greater Kailash I
New Delhi 110 048 India

Printed in the United States of America

Library of Congress Catalog Card No. 89-043409

Bourque, Linda Brookover, 1941-
    Processing data: the survey example / Linda B. Bourque, Virginia A. Clark.
       p.   cm.—(A Sage university papers series. Quantitative applications in the social sciences; v. 85)
    Includes bibliographical references.
    ISBN 0-8039-4741-0 (pbk.)
    1. Social sciences—Data processing.   I. Clark, Virginia, 1928-
II. Title. III. Series.
H61.3.B68 1992
300′.285—dc20

92-9653
CIP

96 97 98 99 00 01 10 9 8 7 6 5 4

Sage Production Editor: Judith L. Hunter

When citing a university paper, please use the proper form. Remember to cite the current Sage University Paper series title and include the paper number. One of the following formats can be adapted (depending on the style manual used):

(1) BOURQUE, L. B., and CLARK, V. (1992) Processing Data: The Survey Example. Sage University Paper series on Quantitative Applications in the Social Sciences, 07-085. Newbury Park, CA: Sage.
OR

(2) Bourque, L. B., & Clark, V. (1992) *Processing data: The survey example* (Sage University Paper series on Quantitative Applications in the Social Sciences, series no. 07-085). Newbury Park, CA: Sage.

CONTENTS

SERIES EDITOR'S INTRODUCTION

In this monograph, the notion of data processing is broadly defined to cover the essential steps of quantitative research that must be taken before data analysis can begin. Obviously, these steps determine data quality. Without good data processing, "garbage in, garbage out" is all too likely to hold true. Nevertheless, relatively little is written about proper methods of data preparation, partly because it is more of an "art" when compared with the "science" of hypothesis testing.

Fortunately, Drs. Bourque and Clark, seasoned scientists themselves, have now made the tools of that art more widely accessible. While they have a general interest in the processing of all sorts of social science data—from interviews, observations, records, or documents—the research example upon which they draw most heavily comes from surveys. In particular, surveys of community response to recent California earthquakes, studies carried out under their direction, provide rich illustration.

With respect to designing a questionnaire, the authors discuss key issues. For example, should you create your own instrument, must the items be closed- or open-ended, is a "don't know" category advisable? They provide useful tips as well, such as that responses should be assigned consistent numerical codes, and item categories should be exhaustive and mutually exclusive. In addition, they offer instruction on the complications of such questionnaire and survey elements as "skip patterns" and "heaping."

In terms of data collection, Bourque and Clark spell out the procedures for testing a questionnaire and forming an interview team. On data entry, they give an informative sketch of the old method, batch processing, contrasting it to the current method of interacting with a personal computer. That is, data can be directly entered into the computer, perhaps on a spreadsheet, and analyzed as part of a statistical package, such as SPSS or SAS. To prepare the data for analysis, a data file, or a subfile, may be created. The authors also describe such important data preparation concerns as weighting, casewise versus pairwise deletion, missing values, and transformations. Finally, they offer a summary checklist for study documentation.

Instructors of research methods have a great many texts to select from when they wish to assign something on data analysis. However, on the topic of data processing their choices are few. This comprehensive, up-to-date, readable monograph lengthens that short list. It should be an immense help to all those students who have not yet learned how actually to carry out a research project, but are eager to do so.

—*Michael S. Lewis-Beck*
Series Editor

ACKNOWLEDGMENTS

We would like to thank A. A. Afifi, Beverly Cosand, Philip Costic, Ralph Dunlap, Eve Fielder, Virginia Flack, Carolyn Geda, Linda Lange, Corrie Peek, Susan Sorenson, Elizabeth Stephenson, Terri Walsh, Mel Widawski, and two readers from Sage Publications for their helpful comments and assistance on earlier drafts; Welden Clark for invaluable assistance with Chapter 4; Gloria Krauss for clerical assistance; and Margie Norman, Gloria Krauss, and Ralph Dunlap for editing assistance. Data used in examples were collected and processed with funds from the National Science Foundation (No. 62617 and BCS-9002754), the Natural Hazards Research and Application Center (Purchase Order 494933C1), the Earthquake Engineering Research Institute (EERI M880411), the National Center for Earthquake Engineering Research (Purchase Order R34779), and the Southern California Injury Prevention Research Center under funds from the Centers for Disease Control (No. R49/CCR903622).

PROCESSING DATA
The Survey Example

LINDA B. BOURQUE
VIRGINIA A. CLARK
University of California, Los Angeles

1. INTRODUCTION TO DATA PROCESSING

Data processing is like the backstage of a theater. It is rarely seen and frequently ignored, even by researchers. Few textbooks explain it, and instructors typically give it only passing comment. Yet, just as what goes on behind the scenes greatly contributes to the quality of a stage production, data processing critically affects an investigator's ability to carry out reliable, valid research.

In their haste to test hypotheses, researchers often do a slipshod or incomplete job of data processing. As a result, they may have to process data over and over again to put it into usable form. Such wasted effort eats up time and money budgeted for other things. In the worst cases, researchers may never get their data into a usable form such that their results can be trusted.

In this book, we will explain systematically how to perform data processing using today's technology. The term *data processing* commonly refers to converting verbal or written information into machine-readable data. Under this definition, data processing includes data coding, entering coded data into a computer, verifying data, and conducting range and consistency checks on data files. However, we prefer a broader definition. For us, data processing starts with selecting a data collection strategy and ends when data transformations are complete. This definition includes the following:

- developing response categories for precoded and open-ended questions, and incorporating the categories into the data collection instrument
- collecting the data
- creating data files that can be used by statistical packages such as the Statistical Package for the Social Sciences (SPSS), the Statistical Analysis System (SAS), or BMDP (a program developed for biomedical data)
- transforming data into variables useful for analysis
- documenting all aspects of the study, including the rationale and specifics of coding decisions and transformations

1

All these steps are not covered in equal detail in this volume. Readers who wish further information should refer to the pertinent references provided. This book can be used as a textbook for a course in data processing or as a reference by persons directing or performing data processing.

To set the stage for the chapters that follow: In the remainder of this chapter we briefly discuss what must be considered in choosing a data collection technique, and how this choice influences data processing. Chapter 2 describes the creation of response categories for both precoded and postcoded data. Chapter 3 discusses methods of ensuring accurate data collection. Chapter 4 outlines how data entry and management are combined to create a documented, computer-readable data file. Chapter 5 provides an overview of data transformations used to prepare data for analysis, and of ways to deal with missing data. Chapter 5 also includes a brief discussion of how to evaluate the adequacy of a scale. Chapter 6 discusses the documentation of data processing.

Overview of Data Collection Procedures

Data about people, their institutions, and their activities can be collected *directly*, using questionnaires, interviews, or direct observation, or *indirectly*, from written or electronic records and documents. The method selected is determined by the nature and content of questions that researchers wish to answer, available resources, and accessibility of potential subjects.

QUESTIONNAIRES

Questionnaires are used to collect data that are unavailable in written records or cannot be readily observed. This might include information about attitudes, opinions, and past, present, or anticipated behavior. The *major disadvantage* to the use of questionnaires is that the reliability and validity of data collected depend upon respondents' memories and forthrightness. (See Chapter 3 for a discussion of procedures that can be used to reduce bias and enhance the accuracy of data collection.) Questionnaires can be used only when respondents are available and willing to participate as research subjects. Questionnaires can be filled out by respondents or administered as part of face-to-face or telephone interviews.

In-Person and Telephone Interviews. There are *major advantages* to using interviews: Researchers can collect more information, and more complex information, from more subjects; based upon the requirements of the study, interviewers can select respondents and control the order in which data are obtained; and "skip patterns" can be set up (see Chapters 2, 4, and 5) to tailor questionnaires to respondents with different experiences, opinions, or attitudes. The cost of training, paying, and supervising interviewers is the *major disadvantage* of both in-person and telephone interviews. Telephone interviews are less costly than face-to-face interviews, but they restrict the pool of subjects to those who live in households with phones.

Since interviews allow for longer and more complex data collection, *data processing* of interviews is likely to take longer and to cost more. The volume of data collected for each respondent may vary widely when skip patterns are used to allow for differences among respondents. This creates special challenges during data entry and processing. On the other hand, the use of interviewers can reduce the amount of unexplained missing data (see Chapter 5). The increased availability of computer-assisted telephone interviewing (CATI) and computer-assisted personal interviewing (CAPI) can greatly simplify data entry and the data processing that precedes analysis (see Aday, 1989).

Self-Administered Questionnaires. Self-administered questionnaires can be used with or without the researcher's presence. Mailed questionnaires are the most common example of interviews administered outside the presence of the researcher. Questionnaires distributed to classrooms of students are probably the most common example of researcher-supervised, self-administered questionnaires. Self-administered questionnaires are briefer, less complex, and more highly structured than interviewer-administered questionnaires. In general, questions in self-administered questionnaires should be "closed-ended," requiring, for example, yes, no, or multiple-choice responses, rather than "open-ended," requiring responses such as "fill in the blanks" or subjective narratives (see Chapter 2).

The *major advantage* of self-administered mail questionnaires is that there is no need to train and supervise interviewers who must then locate and interview subjects. This substantially reduces the time and money spent on data gathering. All study participants can be sent the questionnaire on the same day or given the instrument to fill out on a given day at a given location.

The *major disadvantage* of mailed questionnaires is the low and differential response rate. Uninterested persons fail to return questionnaires, illiterate respondents cannot participate, and out-of-date or inaccurate address lists prevent questionnaires from reaching targeted persons. Lack of control is also a problem. Although self-administered questionnaires usually are sent to a specific individual, once sent, there is no guarantee that the questionnaire will be completed by the designated person.

Data may be missing because respondents only partially complete what seem to them to be lengthy, repetitive, or incomprehensible questionnaires. When questionnaires are administered to groups of respondents, the respondents' perceptions of the researcher or the location (e.g., a clinic or a church) may cause them to change their answers to fit their perceptions of the responses desired. Researchers can reduce some of these problems by restricting the use of mail questionnaires to literate, highly motivated populations, by careful pilot testing, and by utilizing a variety of follow-up techniques to increase response rates (Dillman, 1978).

Special data processing is often needed because of the considerable amount of missing data (see Chapter 5), or because unsupervised respondents do not follow instructions on precoded questionnaires (see Chapter 4). On the other hand, the elimination of skips from self-administered questionnaires and the use of closed-ended questions simplify data entry and the creation of data files (see Chapter 4). In addition, respondents sometimes can be asked to record answers directly on scannable sheets, which greatly facilitates computer entry.

OBSERVATION

Observation can be either a direct or an indirect form of data collection. Subjects under observation may or may not be aware of being observed. Webb, Campbell, Schwartz, and Suchrest (1966) provide one of the best discussions available on the use of unobtrusive, indirect observational methods. Spradley (1980), Scrimshaw and Hurtado (1987), and Miles and Huberman (1984) discuss direct, overt observation in which the emphasis is on observing whether events occur, how they occur, with what timing, and in what order. Observations are frequently used to study interactions between people, and between people and their environment.

Videotapes, audiotapes, event recorders, or data collection forms can be used alone or in combination to collect observational data. When tapes are used, data must be transcribed and "content analyzed" prior to analysis (see Chapter 2). Data collection forms differ considerably depending on what is being observed and on the level of detail desired, but carefully structured, precoded forms can help the observer focus on what is to be observed, rather than on the mechanics of filling out the form.

The *major advantage* of direct observation is that the researcher directly observes events rather than relying on the respondent's memory or truthfulness in reporting. The *major disadvantages* are that observation is time-consuming and can be used only when the information desired is readily amenable to observation. As a result, samples of people or events frequently are small and unrepresentative. It is difficult to replicate direct observations and, like inter-viewers, observers must be carefully trained and monitored so that data are accurately and reliably recorded, both across observers and over time.

In many studies, more than one observer must be used. A preliminary study may be undertaken to determine if significant differences exist among the observers' ratings prior to beginning the main study. For a discussion of the design and analysis of such a study using continuous or equal interval data, see Fleiss (1986); for categorical data, see Fleiss (1981). (See Chapter 2 for our definition of interval data.) The results of the analyses can be used to determine whether it is best to retrain or drop one or more observers, stratify on observers in the analyses, use more than one observer for each observation, or proceed with the study. Often the problem can be avoided by having training sessions at which all the observers are present and differences in rating are discussed. As the study progresses, these analyses should be repeated at intervals to determine whether the observers are drifting out of agreement.

Special data processing requirements frequently include the need to manipulate large amounts of data for very few people. The length and content of data files often are not uniform and, when information is missing, it is difficult to know if a behavior did not occur or was not recorded. When the sample size is small or the behaviors observed simple, data processing may be performed more efficiently by hand than by computer.

RECORDS

Institutional records and other documents provide a major indirect source of data on people. Institutional records are developed by the government, educational institutions, corporations, the armed forces, and many other groups for a wide variety of reasons. Examples include the U.S. Census, work records, medical records, birth and death certificates, school records, and coroner's reports. Appointment and intake logs for medical or other facilities provide examples of less permanent records that may be used as a source of data.

The *major advantage* of records is their availability. When records are available in a centralized location, data collection is often cheaper and fewer cases may be missing. Records allow access to persons who are no longer available because of death or migration and allow the retrieval of information on events, such as immunizations, that a respondent may be unable to remember adequately or accurately. If it can be assumed that data were recorded uniformly across people, records provide an unbiased source of data.

From the researcher's point of view, the *major disadvantage* of records is that typically they are not collected for research purposes. This means that the data of interest may not exist or, if they do exist, they may be incomplete or not in readily usable form. Moreover, because data may have been collected by numerous people with differing levels of competence and interest, it may be difficult to establish the accuracy of the information. Finally, researchers may need to spend a great deal of time or may have difficulty gaining access to data they wish to use.

Data processing requirements vary widely when records are used as the source of information. Sometimes data must be collected by hand using forms similar to a questionnaire (see Chapter 2). However, if records are computerized, researchers may not have to do any data collection or data entry at all, which makes data processing quite simple. On the other hand, if very limited data are to be extracted from a large data file, large amounts of missing data or irregular files may add to the data processor's problems. In cases where information is to be collected from multiple computer files with different kinds of identifying information, and the researcher wishes to employ secondary data from several sources or to integrate secondary data with primary data, specialized computer expertise may be needed (see Brewer & Hunter, 1989; Hyman, 1972; Kiecolt & Nathan, 1985). Merging data sets is a common problem in such research.

Data Collection Techniques: Sources

Readers interested in more detailed information about data collection techniques may want to read some of the excellent publications on the subject. The following authors, among others, can provide a more in-depth understanding of the topic: Adams and Preiss (1960), Aday (1989), Alwin (1991), Boone and Wood (1992), Bradburn and Sudman (1979), Converse and Presser (1986), Dillman (1978), Fink and Kosecoff (1985), Hall (1966), Jobe and Loftus (1991), Miles and Huberman (1984), Patton (1990), Scrimshaw and Hurtado (1987), Sheatsley (1983), Spradley (1980), Stewart and Kamins (1993), Sudman and Bradburn (1982), and Webb et al. (1966).

Data Processing by Example: Earthquake Research

The remainder of this book will explain and describe data processing by example. Two surveys of community response to earthquakes that we have recently completed will serve as the primary source of our examples. Although our examples are drawn from studies of people, many of the data processing steps discussed are relevant to other kinds of data.

Both studies used similar questionnaires to collect data through telephone interviews lasting approximately 30 minutes each. All interviews were conducted by staff of the Institute for Social Science Research, University of California, Los Angeles.

The first study examined community behavior during and after the Whittier Narrows earthquake of October 1, 1987, which measured 5.9 on the Richter scale. Data were collected from 690 adult residents of Los Angeles County. The second study occurred approximately two years later in response to the Loma Prieta earthquake of October 17, 1989, of 7.1 magnitude. The slightly fewer (656) respondents in the second study were residents of five counties in the San Francisco Bay Area.

To reflect the normal progress and problems often associated with data processing during the course of conducting survey research, we discuss what worked, what did not work, and what could have been improved in our earthquake studies. We also indicate how our experiences during the Whittier Narrows study helped us modify and improve the Loma Prieta study.

2. DESIGNING FORMS FOR DATA COLLECTION

This chapter covers the design of data collection forms. First we describe types of data that can be collected, selection of variables, and how future analytical needs influence the format of a data collection form. Next we discuss how data collection forms used by other researchers can be adapted or adopted for use in current work, and differences between open- and closed-ended questions. We demonstrate how the format of a data collection form can facilitate computer entry, describe the development of response categories for closed-ended questions, and show how skip patterns and other characteristics of forms can influence data. In the final section we explain how to develop code frames for open-ended responses.

General Characteristics of Data Collection Forms

To gather accurate information to test theories or hypotheses, data collection forms must be reliable, systematic, and complete. To simplify the work of data collectors and ensure consistent and accurate use of forms, instruments must be self-explanatory, freestanding, and comprehensive. Persons who use them should not be expected to shuffle among several forms or be forced to refer to other documents while completing a form. A well-designed form will enable different data collectors to interview or observe in such a way that each will obtain identical information from a given respondent, record, or unit of analysis.

IDENTIFICATION NUMBER

Every respondent, case, or unit of analysis in your study must have a unique identification number. Names should not be used as identification because that would breach confidentiality. The simplest way is to assign ID numbers in sequence as data collection forms are returned to a central office, but often it is useful to embed information about the sample within the identification number.

TYPES OF DATA TO COLLECT

One of the worst things that can happen during the course of research is to arrive at the analysis stage and suddenly discover that you failed to collect an essential piece of information. To minimize chances of this happening, you should keep in mind the five types of information that may be collected: information about the respondent and information about his or her environment, behaviors, experiences or status, and thoughts or feelings. The first type is frequently referred to as *demographic data*. These data usually include gender, age, educational level, income, employment, marital status, ethnic or racial background, religion, and sometimes housing type. Novice researchers most often forget to collect information on one or more of these important demographic variables.

The other four types of data, alone or together, are usually the focus of research. Most commonly, studies are interested in two or more of these four types. For example, to assess the strength of opinions and attitudes, ordinarily it is also useful to know something about respondents' behavior and/or environment.

KEEPING YOUR ANALYSIS NEEDS IN MIND

It is important to keep analysis needs in mind while designing the data collection form. When there is uncertainty or when data can be collected in a variety of ways, it is best to collect them as interval data. By *interval data*, we mean continuous data that have equal intervals such that the difference between 1 and 2 always equals the difference between 2 and 3. From interval data, statistics such as the mean, standard deviation, and correlation can be interpreted.

Adopting, Adapting, or Developing
a Data Collection Form

Researchers do one of three things when they develop a data collection form: *adopt* items developed by other researchers, *adapt* items developed by other researchers, or *develop* their own items. Obviously, it is most efficient to adapt or adopt pertinent sections of existing instruments. This also is essential when the objective of the research is to replicate another study or to use findings from another study as a standard.

ADOPTING INSTRUMENTS DEVELOPED BY OTHERS

Generally, there are five reasons that encourage researchers to adopt items from other studies. One is to replicate a study's findings on another population or at a later date. Another is when an investigator feels he or she cannot improve on another's instrument.

Adopting rather than adapting is also done when the desired instrument is under copyright, which assures the author that it cannot be used or changed without his or her permission. In the earthquake studies we used the Brief Symptom Inventory (BSI) to assess psychological well-being (Derogatis & Spencer, 1982) and the Mississippi Scale—Revised to assess levels of post-traumatic stress disorder (PTSD) (Keane, Caddell, & Taylor, 1988). Before we could use these instruments, however, we contacted the researchers who designed them, described what we intended to do, received permission, and paid fees to use the BSI. Even if a formal copyright does not exist, research ethics dictate that you document where you obtained the instrument and give credit to the original researcher.

A fourth reason a researcher may adopt items is to compare his or her study population with subjects used in other studies. The final motivation is to use instruments of known reliability and validity, to save the time and expense associated with constructing a new instrument.

In any case, when a researcher adopts items or sets of items from other researchers, no changes should be made in wording, answer categories, order or format of questions, or administrative procedures.

Selecting Items to Adopt. There are two major ways to go about finding items to include in a study. One is to be familiar with other research being conducted in the field, and the other is to consult one of the many books that contain lists of questions and summarize information on their prior use (e.g., Chun, Cobb, & French, 1975; George & Bearon, 1980; Kane & Kane, 1981; McDowell & Newell, 1987; Reeder, Ramacher, & Gorelnik, 1976; Robinson, Rusk, & Head, 1973; Robinson & Shaver, 1973; Robinson, Shaver, & Wrightsman, 1991; Shaw & Wright, 1967).

ADAPTING INSTRUMENTS DEVELOPED BY OTHERS

If any aspect of an instrument is changed, the instrument is considered adapted rather than adopted. Adaptation occurs for a variety of reasons: Some instruments are too long to be included in their entirety; a population other than the original population is being studied; instruments may need to be translated into other languages; or researchers may need to expand, reorder, or otherwise elaborate on items or change the procedure by which data are collected—for instance, an item written for an in-person interview may be modified for a mail questionnaire. If modifications are made in an instrument, pilot testing should be repeated and the instrument's reliability and validity must be reevaluated.

Adapting Turner, Nigg, and Heller Paz (1986). Questionnaires used in our earthquake research were adapted primarily from Turner et al. (1986). As part of their series of studies on earthquake predictions, Turner and his colleagues designed a questionnaire to be administered only when an earthquake of a certain size occurred. While they never used the instrument, our ability to adapt it saved us considerable time and expense. We could not adopt it in its entirety, however, because our research objectives were somewhat different from theirs, and we wanted to restrict our telephone interviews to 30 minutes each.

The major change we made was to create open-ended questions from closed-ended questions. Figure 2.1 shows a question as it was originally written, how we first modified it for the Whittier Narrows study, and then how we adapted it again for the Loma Prieta study.

Originally Turner had provided three answers for the question, "What kind of damage was this?" Each respondent who reported damage was asked whether

A. Question as Written by Turner et al. (1986)

16. Was the home you were living in damaged enough to need repairs?

YES .... ASK A 1
NO .... SKIP TO B 2

  A. What kind of damage was this? Was it:

Major structural damage 1
Some cracking, but not structural, or 2
Very minor damage, such as objects
   moved around or damaged? 3

B. Question as Adapted for Whittier Narrows Study

12. Was the house you were living in damaged enough to need repairs?

YES .... ASK A 1
NO .... SKIP TO C 2

  A. What kind of damage was this?

_____

_____

C. Question as Revised for Loma Prieta Study

8. Was the home you were living in damaged enough to need repairs, or did you have any *other* personal property or belongings damaged during this earthquake?

YES .... ASK A-K 1
NO .... SKIP TO Q9 2

  A. What kind of damage was this?

Damage to:	CIRCLE ALL THAT APPLY
PERSONAL PROPERTY BROKEN	01
ENTIRE BUILDING DESTROYED	02
FOUNDATION	03
BUILDING OFF FOUNDATION	04
HOUSE WALL(S) DAMAGED	05
HOUSE WALL(S) COLLAPSED	06
CHIMNEY COLLAPSED	07
CEILING/ROOF DAMAGED	08
CEILING/ROOF COLLAPSED	09
WATER PIPES BROKEN	10
WATER HEATER	11
GAS LINES BROKEN	12
FLOORS DAMAGED	13
FLOORS COLLAPSED	14
PATIO/PORCH DAMAGED	15
FENCES/FENCE WALL DAMAGED	16
DRIVEWAY DAMAGED/DESTROYED	17
GARAGE DAMAGED/DESTROYED	18
OTHER	19
SPECIFY: _____	

Figure 2.1. Comparison of Response Categories in Three Studies

he or she experienced "major structural damage," "some cracking, but not structural," or "very minor damage, such as objects moved around or damaged." Because we were not sure how consistent respondents would be in differentiating among these three levels, we deleted the alternative answers and had interviewers record whatever respondents said. These answers were then analyzed for content. As Figure 2.1 shows, the analysis of Whittier Narrows data yielded a rather long list of different kinds of damage. We then used this list as options for answers to the question in the Loma Prieta study.

TYPES OF QUESTIONS

Items in questionnaires can be either open-ended or closed-ended. Similarly, when data are collected by observation or from records, items included on the data collection form are either open-ended or closed-ended.

Open-Ended Questions. Open-ended questions have no lists of possible answers. Questions 1B, 2B, and 4B in Figure 2.2 are open-ended questions that generate brief answers, while Question 3 is an open-ended question that may generate a long and complex answer.

Questions 1B, 2B, and 4B are open-ended because it would be unreasonable to take up enough space to list all possible answers. In contrast, Question 3 is open-ended because the researcher was unsure what kind of answers respondents would give. While open-ended questions are much easier to write than closed-ended items, they generally are more difficult to answer, code, and analyze, because researchers must develop code frames or categories to organize and summarize the collected data. This process is sometimes referred to as *content analysis.*

Closed-Ended Questions. Closed-ended questions contain lists of possible answers from which the respondent selects the answer that best represents his or her view or situation. Questions 1, 1A, 2, 2A, 4, and 4A in Figure 2.2 are closed-ended questions.

When questionnaires are self-administered, respondents select answers to closed-ended questions by circling numbers or checking boxes or spaces. Interviewers administering questionnaires record respondents' answers similarly. Closed-ended questions are much more difficult to design but, if designed carefully and with sufficient pretesting, result in much more efficient data collection, processing, and analysis. Instead of having to write out an answer to the question, the interviewer or respondent selects the word, phrase, or statement from the list of answers that best matches the respondent's answer, the behavior observed if observations are the source of data, or the information available in a record if records are the source of data. When possible, answer categories should be alphabetized using key words.

1. As you probably know, there was an earthquake in Los Angeles on October 1st <u>last</u> <u>year</u>, that was 1987. Did you yourself feel the earthquake on October 1, 1987?

   YES .... SKIP TO Q2 1   V92

   NO .... ASK A 2

   A. Since you did not feel the earthquake, where were you when you found out it had occurred? Were you at:

   <u>CIRCLE ONE ANSWER ONLY</u>

   a. Your own home? .... SKIP TO Q3 1

   b. Someone else's home? ..... ASK B 2

   c. Work? .... ASK B 3

   d. School? .... ASK B 4

   e. Traveling? .... ASK B 5   V93

   f. In a public place? .... ASK B 6

   g. Out of the area? ....SKIP TO C 7

   h. Or somewhere else? .... ASK B 8

   B. What area or city is that in?

   _____

   GEOGRAPHIC LOCATION   V94(2)

   C. When did you first become aware of or hear that this earthquake had occurred?

   SAME DAY 1

   NEXT DAY 2

   FEW DAYS LATER 3

   WEEK LATER 4   V95

   2-3 WEEKS LATER 5

   OTHER 6

          SPECIFY: _____

                   V96

   | SKIP TO PAGE 6, Q8 |

2. When the earthquake struck, were you:

   Indoors, or 1   V97

   Outdoors? 2

   A. Where were you when the earthquake struck? Were you at:

   <u>CIRCLE ONE ANSWER ONLY</u>

   a. Your own home? .... SKIP TO Q3 1

   b. Someone else's home? ..... ASK B 2

   c. Work? .... ASK B 3

   d. School? .... ASK B 4   V98

   e. Traveling on a road
      or freeway? .... ASK B 5

   f. In a public place like a
      building or store? .... ASK B 6

   g. Or somewhere else? .... ASK B 7

Figure 2.2. Creation of Precoded, Closed-Ended Questions

B. What area or city is that in?

GEOGRAPHIC LOCATION	V99(2)

3. When you felt the earthquake, what was the very <u>first</u> thing you did?

_____

_____
V100(4)

4. When the earthquake struck, were you:
    Alone, or .... SKIP TO Q5 1   V101
    With others? .... ASK A 2

    A. Who were you with?

    CIRCLE ALL MENTIONS

    ADULTS IN MY HOUSEHOLD
       (OTHER THAN CHILDREN) 1   V102
    CHILDREN IN HOUSEHOLD 18 YRS
       AND OVER 1   V103
    CHILDREN IN HOUSEHOLD 17 YRS
       AND UNDER 1   V104
    OTHER RELATIVES NOT PART OF
       HOUSEHOLD 1   V105
    CO-WORKERS 1   V106
    FRIENDS/NEIGHBORS 1   V107
    OTHERS 1   V108
       SPECIFY: _____
    V109(2)

    B. Not counting yourself, how many <u>other</u> people were you with?
        (RECORD AS GIVEN.)   _____
        V110(4)

Figure 2.2. Continued

Facilitating Direct Computer Entry

Figure 2.2 presents a questionnaire that was set up to facilitate direct computer entry. Note that most questions are closed-ended, and many of the open-ended questions (e.g., 1B) require only brief answers. Moreover, all closed-ended questions have been precoded: A unique number has been assigned to each possible answer. The interviewer, data collector, or respondent simply circles the number corresponding to the answer selected. These codes are then used to enter data into the computer for analysis. Precoding simplifies answer selection and forces the researcher to decide in advance how data will be organized and coded for data entry and analysis. Computer-assisted telephone interviewing systems also facilitate direct entry of data into computers (Frey, 1989).

To reduce errors, answers in the questionnaire shown in Figure 2.2 are listed vertically, with dotted lines guiding the user to corresponding answer options. Researchers sometimes list answers horizontally in order to save space, but this significantly increases the chances for error. For instance, in the example below it would be easy for a respondent who wished to answer yes to check the line *after* rather than *before* the yes. His or her selection would then be incorrectly tallied as a no.

Did you yourself feel the earthquake on October 1, 1987?

    _____ Yes   _____ No

In the questionnaire represented in Figure 2.2, to mimic the way our eyes travel from left to right while reading English, codes are placed to the right of each alternative and lined up vertically on the right-hand side of the page. Because all answers are located on the right and answer categories are not mixed in with text, it is easy for data collectors or respondents to record answers; this layout also facilitates transfer of answers to a computerized data base.

Developing Response Categories for Closed-Ended Questions

Listed below are rules that should be followed when designing answers for closed-ended or precoded questions and when devising data collection forms that contain those answers.

1. Answer categories should be exhaustive; that is, they should represent the full range of possible answers.
2. Answer categories should be mutually exclusive.
3. Answer categories should be designed to make it easy for data collectors, respondents, or coders to select appropriate options.
4. Answer categories should include a residual "other" option, with sufficient space for writing answers that were not anticipated.
5. Answer categories should anticipate analytical needs and enable the collection of data that are suitable for those analyses.
6. Open-ended questions should be used if they will provide interval data that closed-ended questions will not.
7. Consistent conventions should be used to record when data are unavailable and, when appropriate, to indicate the reasons data are missing.
8. Consistent codes for identical answers should be used throughout the instrument.

9. Codes that minimize transformations during analysis and correspond to everyday meanings of answers should be used throughout the instrument.

10. If the study will employ interviewers, it should be decided whether or not they will read aloud alternative answers to closed-ended questions.

11. It should be decided whether single or multiple answers are to be allowed, and consistent corresponding codes should be created.

12. Instructions on how to complete the form should be provided; whether and how skip patterns should be used should be carefully considered.

Due to ignorance, haste, or egocentrism, researchers frequently violate one or more of these rules. One of the most common mistakes is to assume that you know the range of possible responses and how to differentiate among them. Pilot studies and pretests will help you avoid these problems (see Frey, 1989).

In general, as solutions are created for one rule violation, at least a partial solution is provided for some others. As the following examples show, if answer categories really are exhaustive and mutually exclusive, they probably include a residual "other" category and are easy for respondents, interviewers, and coders to use.

EXHAUSTIVE RANGE OF RESPONSES

The following question from the Loma Prieta earthquake questionnaire failed to provide an exhaustive list, a residual "other," and, for some respondents, a mutually exclusive list.

5. Did you turn on or find a TV or radio to get more information about the earthquake?

```
YES, REGULAR TV ...................... 1
YES, BATTERY TV ...................... 2
YES, REGULAR RADIO .................. 3
YES, BATTERY RADIO .................. 4
NO ..................................... 5
```

We thought our list of answers was both exhaustive and mutually exclusive, so we did not include a residual "other" category in our list of answers. We discovered that we had failed to consider car radios. Many people reported that they were in cars at the time of the earthquake and turned on car radios to get information. We discovered our error during the pretest and were able to tell interviewers to add this answer to the list of possibilities. Including a residual "other," so that the interviewer could write down "car radio," would also have solved this problem.

Impact of Incomplete Lists on Data Quality. Generally, investigators end up with incomplete lists of categories because they have failed to examine questions developed by others or do not pretest instruments carefully enough. If a residual "other" category is included in an incomplete or poorly constructed list, a considerable number of respondents, interviewers, or coders will use it. This means investigators must later code what has essentially become an open-ended question. If no residual "other" category is provided, the respondent or interviewer may choose the single category that is closest to the desired response. This may result in lost information or in frequency distributions that "heap" or concentrate respondents in a single response category.

Heaping. An example of heaping occurred in the Whittier Narrows study when respondents were asked about their family income in 1987. Each respondent was asked to select the category that contained his or her family's income. We used prior Los Angeles County studies as our guide, and the top category we provided was "Over $40,000." However, the average family income in Los Angeles County increased rapidly during the 1980s, so when we started to analyze the data we found significant heaping of subjects in this highest category; 38% of our respondents reported family incomes over $40,000. As a result, we did not have a very clear idea of the distribution of family income in Los Angeles County.

Lost Data. The following question on marital status provides an example of an incomplete list that resulted in lost data.

47. What is your current marital status?
    NEVER MARRIED 1
    MARRIED 2
    DIVORCED 3
    SEPARATED 4
    WIDOWED 5

Although unmarried cohabitation is increasingly common throughout the United States, our question on marital status did not allow respondents to report cohabitation, so data about living arrangements were lost. Clearer specification of why we wanted information on marital status would have prevented this problem from occurring. If our objective was to obtain information about legal marital status, the question as written was sufficient. If, however, we also wished to find out about respondents' current living arrangements, additional questions should have been included.

MUTUALLY EXCLUSIVE ANSWERS AND EASILY USED CATEGORIES

The process of creating mutually exclusive answer categories overlaps with creating categories that are easy for the respondent, data collector, or coder to use. Figure 2.2 shows that Question 3 as posed in the Whittier Narrows study was open-ended. After analyzing the content of those data, we closed the question for the Loma Prieta study using categories of answers that resulted from the Whittier analysis:

```
GOT UNDER DOORWAY/TABLE/COVER  ............10
FROZE/STAYED WHERE WAS  ......................11
CAUGHT FALLING OBJECTS  ......................12
RAN OUTSIDE  .....................................13
WENT TO CHILD  ..................................14
CALLED INSTRUCTIONS TO OTHERS IN AREA  .......15
PULLED CAR OVER  ...............................16
CONTINUED DRIVING  ............................17
OTHER  ............................................18
     SPECIFY:_____
```

Our new list turned out to be exhaustive, but not always mutually exclusive. Many respondents reported doing several things, so interviewers had difficulty figuring out the *first* thing they did. Respondents might say they stayed where they were and called to others in the area, or that they grabbed a child and went to a door frame. In these instances, interviewers ignored the problem by acting as if the question were still open-ended and writing out everything respondents said.

INCLUDING A RESIDUAL "OTHER" CATEGORY

The lists of answers for Questions 1C and 4A in Figure 2.2 include a residual "other" category with space for the interviewer to write in responses not included on the answer list. We point this out to reiterate our belief that in general, researchers should always include a residual "other" category in the list of response alternatives to closed-ended questions.

ANTICIPATING ANALYTICAL NEEDS
AND USING OPEN-ENDED QUESTIONS

We will consider rules 5 and 6 together. Researchers frequently create closed-ended questions when open-ended questions would provide better data and take up less space. For example, when he wanted information about injuries sustained, Turner asked:

How many were injured? Would you say:
    A few people 1
    Some people, or 2
    Many people? 3

We adapted this question for the Loma Prieta study by making it open-ended:

How many people *in all* do you know who were injured?
    NUMBER OF PEOPLE INJURED: _____

This change had three advantages. First, instead of creating an ordinal variable, we created discrete interval data (e.g., Bailey, 1987). This gave us much more flexibility when we analyzed our data. Second, it took up less space in the questionnaire, and third, it avoided the variable interpretation that results when "vague qualifiers" are used. While some respondents may consider three "a few," others may consider three "some."

Closed-ended questions often are used unnecessarily to collect data that are continuous in character. This error occurs most frequently in self-administered questionnaires. With the possible exception of questions about income, we have little reason to suspect that providing respondents with a list of answers rather than an open-ended question increases the validity of their answers. If the concern is that respondents will hesitate to answer because they don't think they remember the exact number, this can be avoided by instructing them to give their best estimate.

RECORDING MISSING INFORMATION

In the questionnaires shown in Figures 2.1 and 2.2 we have not provided an answer category or code for "don't know" or "no response." Researchers differ regarding the advisability of including such alternatives. Five interrelated issues are raised in discussions about "don't knows." The meaning or value of including a "don't know" category probably differs with the following factors: the researcher's objectives, how data are collected, whether factual or attitudinal information is being solicited, whether respondents are told that a "don't know" category is available, and the extent to which data collectors are trained and monitored. When the researcher's primary objective is to collect factual or behavioral information, we believe it is better not to include "don't know" answers in questionnaires because their existence in a list of alternatives encourages interviewers and respondents to use them when other answers are actually more appropriate. When collection of data on attitudes is the major objective of a study, we recommend that researchers consult the rapidly expanding literature on this topic before making a decision (e.g., Converse, 1970; Duncan & Stenbeck, 1988; Faulkenberry & Mason, 1978; Fieck, 1989; Frey, 1989; Poe, Seeman, McLaughlin, Mehl, & Dietz, 1988; Presser & Schuman, 1989; Sheatsley, 1983). Of course, when such answers are not included, the researcher must provide a way to signify that questions were left unanswered when data are entered into the computer (see Chapter 4).

In contrast, when records or observations are the source of data, we recommend *including* such alternatives in the data collection form. For example, coroner's records contain results from laboratory tests as well as notes recorded by the coroner. If test results are important to the study, then the data collection form should clearly *identify* which tests are to be examined, *specify* what data are to be recorded about each test, and include a way to indicate that a given person's file contains *no record* of that particular test.

Probably one of the biggest errors made in extracting data from records is failing to note that a recorder looked for a piece of information and did not find it. To correct this, instead of merely having a space in which to record results of, for instance, a hemoglobin test, the data form should include a way to indicate that the collector looked for the results but found no indication in the medical record that a hemoglobin test had been run. Without such a category, a blank space can indicate one of two things: Either no test result existed or the data collector missed it.

USING CONSISTENT CODES

Some categories of answers occur repeatedly throughout a data collection instrument, such as yes, no, refused, don't know, missing information, and inapplicable. Researchers can simplify data analysis by using consistent numeric codes throughout the data collection form for these common response options. Figure 2.3 shows the codes we used in the earthquake questionnaires. Yes was always coded 1, no was coded 2, and similarly consistent codes were designed to explain missing answers. For example, if someone was alone when the earthquake struck, obviously the interviewer did not ask the respondent who he or she was with (see Figure 2.2, Question 4A). In this case, the answer was coded 0, for "inapplicable." When respondents said they didn't remember who they were with, a code of 8, designating "don't know," was entered. Respondents who did not want to answer were coded 7 for "refused," and if an interviewer forgot to ask a question and we did not catch the error (see Chapter 3), the answer was coded 9, for "missing data." Depending on the research objectives, a researcher may want to combine or delete codes for missing data in later stages of analysis, but such distinctions should be included in the original data set.

Notice that, with the exception of zeros, the last digit in a field of numbers is used to distinguish among the various missing data codes. This is a convention

Response	Example Code		
	Single Digit	Double Digits	3+ Digits
Yes	1		
No	2		
Refused to answer	7	97	997
Don't know	8	98	998
Missing information	9	99	999
Not applicable	0	00	000

Figure 2.3. Examples of Consistent Codes

that has developed over time. If data were missing for a variable that normally is coded in a field of two or more digits, the "leading digits," all those to the left of the last digit, would be 9s. So, for example, if a respondent refused to give his or her age, age would be given a code of 97; if the question on age was not applicable, it would be coded 00; if it was not asked, it would be coded 99; and if a respondent did not remember (or claimed not to remember) his or her age, it would be coded 98. Of course, when a study is focused on an elderly population, the researcher might want to use three digits in coding age to ensure that the codes for respondents aged 90 and above are not confused with the codes used for missing data. In such a case, codes of 997 and 998 would be used for instances where respondents refused or did not know their age.

CODES THAT MINIMIZE TRANSFORMATIONS
DURING DATA ANALYSIS

Researchers frequently assign codes to answer categories arbitrarily, without thinking about how codes might facilitate later analysis of the data. For example, if one possible response to a question is "none," why not use zero as the code? In the earthquake questionnaires, respondents were asked whether their homes were damaged as a result of the earthquake. Respondents who reported damage were then asked to estimate the amount of damage in dollars. Consistent with our earlier suggestion to design open-ended questions when potential answers have a continuous range, we made this an open-ended question. This question was coded 0, connoting *inapplicable* for persons who experienced no damage. Codes for persons who reported damage were the dollar amounts entered as responses to the open-ended question. Thus when we analyzed the data we did not have to transform it; persons who reported no damage already were coded 0, and costs for those who did report damage were coded by the amount of damage reported.

ARE ALTERNATIVE ANSWERS TO BE READ TO RESPONDENTS?

When data are collected by interview, the researcher must decide whether or not the interviewer will read alternative answers to the respondent. In general, if the researcher wants a respondent to be aware of all the alternative answers or wants to maximize the accuracy of the respondent's recollections and the reporting of behaviors and attitudes, he or she will have the list read to the respondent. In face-to-face interviews, cards that list the possible alternatives are sometimes handed to the respondent. Lists of answers are *not* read to the respondent when doing so would be redundant with the question, or when the researcher does not want to "lead" the respondent by suggesting answers to him or her.

In Questions 1 and 2 in Figure 2.2, there was no reason for the interviewer to read "yes" and "no" or "indoors" and "outdoors" to the respondent because the answer alternatives essentially duplicate the substance of the question. In Questions 1A and 2A, however, the possible answers *were* read to the respondent and the respondent was asked to choose the single answer that best described where he or she was at the time of the earthquake.

In Question 3, we wanted respondents to tell us what they did during the earthquake without their obtaining any suggestions or "cues" from us regarding what we think they should have done. Thus the alternative answers reported earlier, which were created from the Whittier Narrows data for inclusion in the Loma Prieta questionnaire, were *not* read to respondents.

On our questionnaires, we differentiate between answers that are to be read to respondents and those that are not to be read: When answers are to be read to a respondent they are in lowercase type; when answers are only for the interviewer to use, they are in uppercase type.

WILL SINGLE OR MULTIPLE ANSWERS BE ALLOWED?

When creating closed-ended questions, it is important to decide whether respondents will be encouraged to give multiple answers to a question or be restricted to a single answer. In Question 4A in Figure 2.2, respondents were encouraged to report all the different kinds of people they were with at the time of the earthquake. In contrast, in Questions 1A, 2A, and 3, respondents were asked to provide a single answer.

When a list of alternative answers is included in a data collection form or questionnaire, the instructions must clarify whether single or multiple answers are desired. For example, in Questions 1A and 2A we state, "CIRCLE ONE ANSWER ONLY," while in Question 4A we state, "CIRCLE ALL MENTIONS." In concert with those instructions, the number of variables created from each answer shows whether single or multiple answers are intended; a single variable, V98, is assigned to Question 2A, while seven variables (one for each alternative response) are assigned to Question 4A.

12. Was the home you were living in damaged enough to need repairs?

    YES ....ASK A 1

    NO .... SKIP TO C 2

A. What kind of damage was this?

_____

_____

B. Was the damaged caused by: (CIRCLE ALL THAT APPLY)

    The earthquake itself on Oct. 1, or 1

    By aftershocks?.............................1

    OTHER 1

    SPECIFY: _____

C. Did you have any other personal property or belongings damaged during this earthquake?

    YES ....ASK D 1

    NO .... SKIP TO Q13 2

D. What is your estimate of the amount of damage to your home and property? (RECORD DOLLAR AMOUNT. PROBE FOR BEST ESTIMATE).

    DOLLAR AMOUNT: _____

E. Have you applied for disaster assistance?

    YES .... ASK F 1

    NO .... SKIP TO Q13 2

F. How much did you apply for?

    DOLLAR AMOUNT: _____

G. Have you received disaster assistance?

    YES ....ASK H 1

    NO .... SKIP TO Q13 2

H. How much assistance did you receive?

    DOLLAR AMOUNT: _____

Figure 2.4. Example of Skip Patterns

CREATING SKIP PATTERNS

The ability to create "skip patterns" is one of the most powerful features of data collection. These logical branches allow researchers to customize instruments for different kinds of respondents. We must point out, however, that creating good skip patterns is a difficult task. Even when well-designed skip patterns are used, it is still possible to gather incomplete data that will complicate the creation of variables useful for analysis.

In the Whittier Narrows study we asked respondents, "Was the home you were living in damaged enough to need repairs?" (see Question 12 in Figure 2.4).

Persons who answered yes were asked about the kind of damage suffered and its cause (see Questions 12A and 12B in Figure 2.4); persons who answered no were *not* asked these two questions and were "skipped" to Question 12C. *Both* groups of respondents were asked, "Did you have any *other* personal property or belongings damaged during this earthquake?" (see Question 12C in Figure 2.4). Persons who answered yes to this question were then asked to estimate the dollar amount of their damage and whether they applied for disaster assistance (see Questions 12D-12H); persons who answered no were skipped to the next section of the questionnaire.

When we designed the questionnaire, the logic of our skip pattern looked fine to us, but when we started analyzing our data we discovered a major logical flaw. A total of 85 people in this study reported damage to their homes, while 605 people reported no damage to their homes. In contrast, 120 people reported damage to personal property, while 534 people reported no damage to personal property. Our skip pattern assumed that *all respondents who reported damage to their homes would report damage to personal property!* In fact, 36 of the 85 people with damage to their homes reported no damage to personal property. Because our assumptions did not allow for this combination of responses, these 36 people were not asked to estimate the dollar amount of their damage or whether they sought disaster assistance. The problem caused by this particular sequence of skip patterns led to missing data for these 36 people that had to be estimated prior to analysis (see Chapter 5).

A simple flow diagram can help verify that the branching and skipping in a data collection instrument work as intended. Had we tested our design when we created the questions in Figure 2.4, we might have caught our error. Parts A and B of Figure 2.5 show how to develop a flow diagram using the material from questionnaire fragments included in Figures 2.2 and 2.4. They also document the structure of the data collection instrument.

In Figure 2.5, the questions for which responses are to be obtained are shown as rectangular boxes. Each major question is placed at the head of a column, with subsidiary questions below it. Changes in flow, based on the response to a question, are shown by diamond-shaped decision boxes directly below the question. Thus in part A of the figure a "yes" response to Question 1 results in transfer directly to Question 2, while a "no" response continues the flow through the subquestions of Question 1.

There is one basic difference between the two parts of Figure 2.5. The structure in part A (from Figure 2.2) is one of "branching," with a substantial series of subsequent questions on each subsequent branch. In contrast, the structure in part B (from Figure 2.4) is primarily one of "skipping" subordinate questions while continuing along one general track. Thinking about this distinction helps clarify how to structure a particular line of questioning. (Both of these structures are referred to as *networks*, in that they branch out and then rejoin, in contrast to a *tree*, where branches do not rejoin.)

A. Illustration of Skip "Branching" Pattern

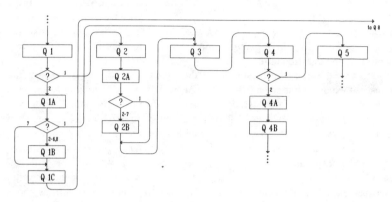

B. Illustration of Skip Pattern

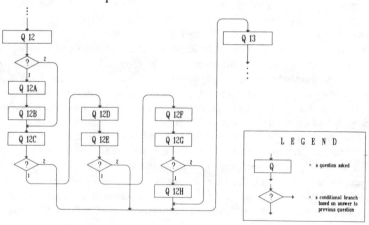

Figure 2.5. Flow Diagrams of Skip Patterns in the Questionnaire Fragments Presented in Figures 2.2 and 2.4

Developing Code Frames for Open-Ended Questions

When open-ended questions are used to collect data, verbal answers must be postcoded or content analyzed. During this process, text is transformed into numbers. This is similar to, but briefer than, what is done when newspapers and other publications are summarized for analysis (e.g., Weber, 1985).

SHORT OPEN-ENDED ANSWERS

Earlier we noted that questions may be left open to save space otherwise taken up by lengthy lists of options, because better-quality data are obtained, or because the researcher is unsure what the range and variety of answers should be. In the simplest example of the first case, coding involves creating a list of answers given, arbitrarily assigning number codes to the list, and recording codes for each respondent's answers. In the simplest example of the second case, coding involves recording a number that was given in response to a question asking, for example, the respondent's age.

Sometimes, however, seemingly simple open-ended questions of this sort require the researcher to develop more complicated answers; for example, Question 4B, "Not counting yourself, how many *other* people were you with?" While most respondents gave a single number, such as 1 or 5, respondents who were at work, in stores, or in other public places sometimes gave ranges, such as 20-25, or verbal answers, such as "a lot." In these cases, we decided to select the midpoint of the range given and round up to the nearest integer. The person who said 20-25 was given a code of 23. The answer "a lot" was arbitrarily given a code of 95. Regardless of *what* the decision is, once a decision is made, the researcher must carefully document the new "coding rule" and use it consistently throughout the remainder of the coding process. (For a thorough discussion of editing procedures and coding rules, see Sonquist & Dunkelberg, 1977.)

Coding Respondents' Occupations. Information on respondents' occupations frequently is collected using short-answer open-ended questions. In the earthquake studies, respondents were first asked about their current and past employment status. Those who had worked were then asked, "What kind of business, industry, or organization is that?"; "What do/did they make?"; "Is it wholesale, manufacturing, or what?"; "What is/was your main occupation?"; and "What do/did you actually do?" Interviewers did not code the answers. After questionnaires were returned to the central office, answers were coded using the *Alphabetical Index of Industries and Occupations* (U.S. Bureau of the Census, 1982). To maximize accurate coding, information about the industry and the occupation must be available (U.S. Bureau of the Census, 1970; Van Dusen & Zill, 1975). The coder then uses the *Index* to ascertain the appropriate code by assessing information provided about the type of work, the industry or business in which the respondent is employed, and whether or not he or she is self-employed.

Because the above process is relatively time-consuming, and therefore expensive, researchers frequently create less detailed closed-ended questions in which respondents are asked to report whether their jobs are professional, managerial, technical, sales, clerical, craftsman/foreman, service worker, operative, labor (not farm), farm manager, or farm worker.

CREATING A MULTIDIMENSIONAL CODE FRAME
FOR COMPLEX ANSWERS

The most important part of coding open-ended questions is creating a code frame. A code frame shows how verbal answers are converted to numbers. In the above examples and in other, short-answer questions, the creation of the code frame is straightforward and quite simple, but for most open-ended questions the process is more complex. This should come as no surprise, because open-ended questions themselves are designed to obtain information that cannot be summarized adequately in a closed-ended form. In essence, the objective of creating a code frame is to formulate a set of categories that accurately represents answers, and in which each category includes an appreciable number of responses.

The same rules specified earlier to create answer categories for closed-ended questions apply to creating code frames for open-ended questions. As with answer categories, code frames must have exhaustive, mutually exclusive categories that are easy to use. Codes must be meaningful and consistent, should maximize ease of transformation during data analysis, and should adopt the highest form of measurement possible. In addition to the earlier rules, six more must be followed when designing code frames for open-ended questions:

1. Specify the objectives for which the code frame is to be used.
2. Maintain a balance between too much detail and not enough detail.
3. Maximize the maintenance of information.
4. Create a sufficient range of codes, variables, or dimensions so that the coder need not force data into categories.
5. Allow for the systematic coding of missing data.
6. Group together related categories of information and use meaningful leading digits in multidigit codes.

Developing Code Frames: An Example. By analyzing the development of questions concerned with injury in the Whittier Narrows study, we can see how these rules help researchers develop code frames for open-ended questions. Beginning with Question 15, respondents were asked a series of questions about injuries.

ID Number	Answer
074	A headboard fell on a woman on the third floor. . . . She went unconscious.
106	Things fell on me in garage when I went out there.
125	The roof fell in on them and broke the table they were hiding under.
137	Threw me to ground—just had hysterectomy with stitches.
139	Friend's girl was killed when building fell on her at college in East L.A.
160	They sprained their feet as they were running to the doorway.
175	Got hit on head with falling object—Had bump for week.
270	My husband is a cardiologist and his patient had a heart attack—I know the patients slightly.
286	My husband jumped thru the window and suffered a laceration in the heel.
292	The chimney fell down.
327	Me—Mental injury—I came unglued. Dear friend had heart attack. . . . She has no history of heart trouble.

Figure 2.6. Answers to Open-Ended Questions About Injuries, Whittier Narrows Study

15. In this earthquake was anyone you know injured?

    YES . . . . ASK A 1

    NO . . . . SKIP TO Q16 2

    A. Can you tell me about that? Who exactly was this, and how were they injured?

In response to this question, 31 respondents said they knew someone who was injured. Figure 2.6 contains answers given by 11 of these 31 respondents. To include these responses in our study, we had to create a code frame to categorize and analyze these data.

We used all 31 responses to create our code frame. If, in contrast, 500 persons had reported an injury, we would have selected a sample of the 500 responses— possibly 100—to work with in developing our code frame. When creating a code frame, we find it helps to write each answer on an index card. The cards can then be sorted in different ways to determine how many categories are needed to include all responses. We also find it useful for two or more persons to work independently to develop a code frame, and then work together on the final code. This ensures maximum objectivity, validity, and reliability.

Objective of the Code Frame. Usually, answers to an open-ended question can be coded in several ways. For example, when looking at injuries caused by earthquakes, we might be interested in the number of injuries reported, the way an injury occurred, what parts of the body were injured, who (in relation to the respondent) suffered the injury, where it occurred, what the person was doing at the time, whether medical care was sought and obtained, and so on. The amount of detail included in a code

Code Category	Code Value	Number of Respondents
Hit by object	1	11
Cuts	2	3
Sprains, bruises, breaks	3	9
Heart attack	4	2
Don't know	5	1
Trapped	6	1
Other	95	2
Missing	99	2
Not Applicable	0	658
TOTAL		690

Figure 2.7. Simple Code of Injuries

frame is determined by the amount of information respondents give the researcher and what the researcher wants to do with that information. We developed two code schemes for the injury question in the Whittier Narrows study.

Maximizing Information and Encoding Ease. Figure 2.7 shows the first code frame that was developed at the time the data were entered into the computer. Only one variable was created, and each answer was coded into one of its nine categories. Unfortunately, this coding scheme confused how the person was injured (e.g., "hit by an object") with what happened as a result (e.g., "cuts"). Although some respondents gave both kinds of information (see Case 074), the coder was forced to decide which kind of information should be recorded in the machine-readable data set. Furthermore, this coding scheme did not allow us to retrieve information about whether anyone had died from these injuries (see Case 139 in Figure 2.6).

This first scheme is not a good code frame. Answer categories are neither exhaustive nor mutually exclusive, and coders will have difficulty deciding how to code many answers. For example, note that for Case 175, the coder must decide whether the answer is coded 1, for "hit by object," or 3, for "sprains, bruises, or breaks."

As we started analyzing the data, we discovered this single code was both inaccurate and incomplete. Fortunately, because our original answers were stored in a computer file, we were able to develop a new code frame (see Figure 2.8). Instead of coding each answer into one of several categories belonging to a single variable, this time we coded answers into four variables or dimensions. In the new code frame we recorded the *number* of people reported injured, the *identity* of people injured, the *cause* of the injury, and the *type* of injury. Moreover, to maximize information provided, we recorded information on injuries to two different people. "Maximizing information" does not mean the recording of data that do not exist, but it *does* include recording when a piece of information was sought but not found. For example, in this instance, it would

Q15B. You said (. . .) was injured in the earthquake. Can you tell me about that? Who exactly was this, and how were they injured?

Seven 2-digit fields, V512-V518, are set aside to code answers to Q15B. Record the number of injuries reported in Dimension 1 (V512). With the exception of persons who gave an inexact count of injured (e.g., some), the maximum number of injured reported was 2. Code dimensions 2-4 for up to two injured persons or groups. Information for the first injury reported is recorded in variables V513, V515 and V517; information for the second injury is coded in variables V514, V516 and V518.

DIMENSION 1: TOTAL NUMBER REPORTED INJURED (V512: 2 digits)
  None, not applicable 00
  Code number given 01-89
  Some 90
  No information provided on number injured 99

DIMENSION 2: IDENTITY OF INJURED (V513 & V514: 2 digits)
  Respondent 10
  Other household member, unspecified 20
    Spouse 21
    Parent 22
    Child 23
    Sibling 24
    Other relative (aunt, uncle, cousin) 25
    Roommate, friend 26
  Neighbor 30
  Relative, not in household, unspecified 40
    Spouse 41
    Parent 42
    Child 43
    Sibling 44
    Other relative (aunt, uncle, cousin) 45
  Co-worker 50
  Friend, acquaintance 60
  Other 70
  Person not identified 99
  Inapplicable, R knows no one injured 00

DIMENSION 3: CAUSE OF INJURY (V515 & V516: 2 digits)
  Non-structural object(s) fell, unspecified 10
    Pictures 11
    Boxes 12
    Headboard 13
    Light fixture 14
    Broken glass (e.g., dishes, pictures) 15
    Shelves 16
  Parts of structure fell, unspecified 20
    Ceiling tiles 21
    Chimney 22

Figure 2.8. Complex Multidimensional Code for Injuries

DIMENSION 4: INJURY REPORTED (V517 & V518: 2 digits)

Figure 2.8. Continued

mean that the coder sought information about a second injury but no information was provided.

Problems with the first code occurred for two reasons. First, we did not spend enough time discerning how the answers to open-ended questions related to objectives of the study. Second, we fell into the "single-dimension" trap, assuming that a single question can have only one answer. Researchers often assume this, even when multiple coding dimensions would more adequately represent the answers given.

Systematic Recording of Missing Data. In Figure 2.8, the first variable, V512, records the number of injuries reported by the respondent. When no injuries are reported, this variable is "not applicable" and a code of 0 is recorded. When an actual number of injuries is given or can be inferred, the actual number is coded. Respondents 125 and 160 gave general answers and received a code of 90 for "some." Finally, Case 292 gave no information about the number affected, so a 99 was recorded. Later, during analysis, that 99 told us that the coder looked for information about the number of people injured but no information was provided by Case 292. Recording the unavailability of information can be particularly informative when data are taken from records. The remaining three dimensions record information for up to two people reported injured by each respondent.

Grouping Related Categories and Using Meaningful Leading Digits. The second dimension or variable records information about who was injured. Here a two-digit code is used with a meaningful first digit. The codes for persons living in the same household all start with a 2, while codes for relatives outside the household start with a 4. This system enabled us to maintain detailed information in the code frame, while it also made it easy for us to combine categories during later analysis. This code also includes categories for respondents who said they "don't know who was injured," and for respondents who did not tell us who was injured (Case 292).

The third variable coded, V515 (and V516), records the cause of the injury, while the fourth variable, V517 (and V518), records data about the nature of the injury. Again, codes are grouped logically and in some instances include both general and more specific subcodes. We provided a code for persons who said they didn't know what caused the injury or what the injury consisted of as well as for those who did not mention the injury.

Leaving Sufficient Room in a Code Frame. As a rule, code frames are developed from a 20-50% sample of responses. While this gives the researcher a good selection of the total range of responses, some answers may not be represented. Unless properly instructed, coders will frequently try to force such answers into existing codes rather than add new categories. In the current example, we had no category for major burns that could have occurred if a water heater had broken or a gas line had caught fire. Clearly it would not be appropriate to code such burns under 53 for "rug burn," yet a coder might do just that if not instructed to do otherwise.

32

TIMING OF CODE FRAME CONSTRUCTION

Before data entry actually begins, researchers must decide how they will handle answers to open-ended questions. In the past, researchers had to code all open-ended responses at the time that machine-readable data files were created, or had to store the data collection instruments until they had time or needed to code open-ended responses. Microcomputers and data entry software changed all that. Now software programs allow researchers to store answers to open-ended questions in machine-readable files at the same time they convert other precoded data to machine-readable files for analysis. This is a valuable new resource, for, as we saw in our injury example, researchers are not always sure how the responses to open-ended questions should be coded until they have started analysis. Thus it is sometimes better to delay coding of open-ended responses until they are needed in analysis.

3. DATA COLLECTION AND QUALITY CONTROL

The data collection process itself influences the quality of data obtained. No matter how data are collected, the objective is to obtain accurate, complete data that are consistent across respondents, records, or other sources employed. When researchers conduct or supervise data collection, they must develop procedures to monitor its quality; when they hire someone else to do it, that individual or firm will handle most of the tasks discussed in this chapter. Nonetheless, researchers must understand the procedures used so that, where necessary, they can negotiate changes or additions, keeping in mind that such revisions will cost time and money. Careful data collection includes attention to pretesting and pilot studies, hiring and training data collectors, supervising data collectors, and logging and editing completed questionnaires or data collection forms.

Pretests and Pilot Studies

Before a data collection instrument is finalized, it should be pretested or used on a small subsample of the population in a pilot study. We refer to *pretesting* as testing parts of data collection instruments or procedures. This can be done in focus groups, in the laboratory, or out in the field. In a *pilot study* the entire instrument and its administrative procedures are tested in a miniature study. Pilot studies are particularly useful when data will be collected within the context of a larger ongoing activity such as admission to a hospital or attendance at a family planning clinic. In such situations, where investigators usually have received permission to gather data on-site, it is important to coordinate data collection with normal activities of the organization. This minimizes disruption and maximizes cooperation between data collectors and organizational staff.

Many things can be evaluated in a pretest. Researchers may want to learn how well their questions and/or instructions on collection forms are understood, and in what sequence to order data collection. Pretests can reveal how comprehensive response categories are, how adequate a language translation is, how easily and reliably the data collection forms work, how well skip patterns work, and how best to identify, schedule, approach, and follow up on respondents or records. Pretesting can also help a researcher estimate how much the data collection will cost in time and money. We used pilot studies to test how much time it took to collect data from each respondent. Funding restrictions meant we could not allow interviewers to spend more than an average of 30 minutes per interview. After each set of pretests or pilot studies, we deleted unessential questions until we met that requirement.

The persons selected to conduct pretests or pilot studies vary according to the objectives. If the researcher intends to collect the final data personally, he or she should also do the pretesting and pilot work. Often pretests are used during the development of a data collection instrument. Here a pretest or pilot study provides firsthand information about the data collection situation and about problems that can be resolved more easily in this early stage. If other persons conduct pretests or pilot studies, the researcher must monitor or check their work.

In general, if the objective is to identify potential problems and suggest solutions, the best or most experienced data collector should conduct the pretest or pilot. In such cases, the researcher will get the most useful feedback from the pretester whom he or she has instructed to be particularly sensitive to things that do not work or that are being missed by the data collection instrument. When questionnaires are pretested by interview, the researcher may also ask respondents for feedback on how well they understood the instrument or on how easily they were able to complete it. This can be done informally by having the interviewer ask respondents for comments, or more formally by providing questions for the interviewer to ask about respondents' opinions.

It is unwise to use the most experienced interviewers or data collectors in pretests and pilots when the objective is to find out how much time and/or money it will cost to collect data. Obviously, the estimates of such interviewers will understate the difficulties and average time needed for the actual study, in which interviewers with varying levels of experience will be employed (see Aday, 1989; Weinberg, 1983).

Hiring Data Collectors

In general, data collectors must be able to read and write and should have at least a high school education. Advanced education or training may be necessary in some instances, for example, when collecting involves abstracting information from medical records. If data are to be collected by interview, the interviewers selected must have pleasant reading voices, use good diction, and be able to project well enough to be heard and understood easily. Both interviewers and observers must be interested in others, feel comfortable with the subject matter, and appreciate diversity. They also should feel confident about their ability to gather information, yet be able to interact with respondents in ways that do not influence the information they gather. Individuals who are easily shocked by others' attitudes or life-styles, or who try to convince others to accept their view of the world, will not be good interviewers.

Because data collectors often work in the field, away from the research office, they must be good at working alone with only occasional or minimal supervision. Moreover, they must have personalities and temperaments that enable them to get along with persons who control access to data sources and with potential respondents.

There are no restrictions on the age, gender, or race of persons who work with records, and the importance of such characteristics for interviewers is often overemphasized. The general conclusion that can be drawn from research is that the gender and ethnicity of interviewers become relevant only when sexual or ethnic attitudes or behaviors are the object of study (e.g., Anderson, Silver, & Abramson, 1988a, 1988b; Bradburn, 1983; Campbell, 1981; Cotter, Cohen, & Coulter, 1982; Frey, 1989; Reese, Danielson, Shoemaker, Chang, & Hsu, 1986; Schuman & Converse, 1989; Singer, Frankel, & Glassman, 1989; Weeks & Moore, 1981). When found, such effects seem to involve feelings of social deference on the part of the respondent that may more accurately reflect a desire to please the interviewer or differences in age or social class between the interviewer and respondent. Lack of interest in people, personal attitudes about the study's subject matter, and perceptions that information will be difficult to get probably interfere more with an interviewer's ability to conduct an interview than does his or her race, gender, or age.

The single greatest danger in data collection is that the data collector may "lead" the respondent or record data from an interview, record, or observation selectively. Although college students, former missionaries, salespersons, social workers, and nurses may all seem to have the types of experience necessary to be good interviewers, we have found that these persons frequently must unlearn old interpersonal styles before they can become effective interviewers. Giving data collectors thorough training and supervision is the best way to prevent them from leading respondents or gathering selective data. One method is to develop a completely scripted, carefully pretested questionnaire and to train interviewers to stick to it.

Training Data Collectors

Regardless of their past experience, *all* data collectors must be trained. Persons new to data collection need *general* training as well as the *specific* training that even experienced data collectors must receive.

TABLE 3.1
Agenda for Basic Training of Interviewers

1. Presentation of the nature, purpose and sponsorship of the survey
2. Discussion of the total survey process
3. Role of the professional survey interview (including a discussion of ethics of interviewing: confidentiality, anonymity, and bias issues)
4. Role of the respondent (helping respondent learn how to be a respondent)
5. Profile of the questionnaire (identification of types of questions and instructions, answer codes, precolumning numbers for data processing, etc.)
6. Importance and advantages of following instructions (examples of disadvantages to interviewer when instructions are not followed)
7. How to read questions (including correct pacing, reading exactly as printed and in order, conversation tone)
8. How to record answers (for each type of question)
9. How and when to probe (definition and uses of probes for each type of question)
10. Working in the field or on the phone (preparing materials, scheduling work, introduction at the door or on the phone, answering respondent's questions, setting the stage for the interview)
11. Sampling (overview of types of samples, detailed discussion of interviewer's responsibilities for implementation of last stage of sampling on specific survey)
12. Editing (reviewing completed interviews for legibility, missed questions, etc.)
13. Reporting to supervisor (frequency and types of reports required)

SOURCE: "Data Collection: Planning and Management" by E. Weinberg in P. H. Rossi, J. D. Wright, and A. B. Anderson (Eds.) *Handbook of Survey Research*, pp. 344-345. Copyright 1983 by Academic Press. Used with permission.

GENERAL TRAINING

Table 3.1 reproduces Eve Weinberg's (1983) list of items that should be covered when training inexperienced interviewers. Training resources and techniques include written materials, lectures by supervisors, group and individual role playing, practice interviews to be reviewed with the supervisor or in groups with other interviewers, and written exercises.

Most research organizations have training manuals that summarize their training procedures (e.g., Survey Research Center, 1976). We recommend that persons interested in carrying out research obtain copies of such documents and observe training sessions conducted by an experienced research organization. By writing to authors of studies in which data are gathered from records, interested readers may also be able to obtain copies of manuals outlining methods used to train record abstractors.

STUDY-SPECIFIC TRAINING

Specific training focuses on the unique needs of the study in question. The length of training varies with the complexity of the research and past experience of data collectors. If data are to be collected that reveal that subjects are vulnerable to harm from themselves (e.g., suicide) or others (e.g., sexual assault), or that they have harmed or may harm others (e.g., child abuse), data collectors must be taught how to handle such information. If topics are likely to be raised during interviews that may upset interviewers, specialized training and debriefing procedures may need to be developed that allow interviewers to discuss their feelings. When data collection and entry are subcontracted to a full-service survey organization, the researcher and the organization must agree on specifics of the training program.

In the case of the earthquake studies, which employed relatively experienced interviewers, half-day "briefings" were conducted. During training, the objectives of the study were explained and then interviewers were led through the questionnaire using a variety of role-playing techniques. Interviewers were encouraged to ask questions throughout the briefings.

Selecting Respondents. No matter what procedure is chosen to select respondents or records, the data collector must understand and follow it, because this procedure determines characteristics of the sample. If sample selection procedures are not followed exactly, the sample obtained will differ from what was intended.

Debriefing. After the briefing for the Loma Prieta study was completed, interviewers were sent home with lists of telephone numbers generated randomly by the computer. Each interviewer was to complete a minimum of two interviews within a 48-hour period. These were returned immediately to the Institute for Social Science Research for review, and the interviewers were "debriefed." The data collection supervisor discussed with each interviewer his or her experience while interviewing, corrected recording and procedural errors, and ensured that all instructions were followed. In studies employing inexperienced data collectors, researchers may want to arrange practice interviews to give interviewers more experience before their work is assessed by supervisors.

The objective throughout training is to ensure that all data collectors use the questionnaire or data collection instrument as intended. Upon occasion, one may discover that an experienced data collector who has done good work in the past is simply not suited to work on the current study, because of negative or strong attitudes or experiences concerning the topic, or for idiosyncratic situational or personal reasons. (For more information and sources on hiring and training of interviewers, see Aday, 1989; Bradburn, 1983; Weinberg, 1983.)

Supervision During Data Collection

Data collectors must be supervised most closely in the beginning of a study, when they are least experienced in using the instrument and in following study procedures. In this initial stage, the supervisor must verify or validate all completed questionnaires and data collection forms. To verify the accuracy of data collection, the field supervisor recontacts the subject and reconducts all or part of the face-to-face interview. When data are collected by telephone from a central location, supervisors on the premises can monitor actual interviews. When computer-assisted telephone interviewing (CATI) systems are used or data are entered into the computer immediately, the quality of interviewing can also be monitored by conducting analyses of responses to specific questions by the interviewer. If systematic differences are found, they may represent a problem with the quality of the data. (For more information on monitoring of data collectors, see Aday, 1989; Frey, 1989; Weinberg, 1983.)

Abstracted records are verified by supervisors or experienced abstractors who reabstract records. Unfortunately, the only way to verify observations is to have two observers collect data simultaneously. This increases expense, but it does allow the researcher to compare the data obtained across observers and to make empirical estimates of reliability (e.g., Fleiss, 1981, 1986).

Once a data collector is well trained, complete verification is conducted only on a small portion (usually 10%) of his or her interviews or record abstractions, or only when problems are identified as the data are edited or checked. At this stage, verification can involve a complete reinterview or simply the confirmation of demographic information or reported behavior.

Project coordinators or field supervisors are also responsible for monitoring the progress of all interviewers, and for keeping track of all data that have been collected. The "call record" is one way to assess an interviewer's performance.

USING CALL RECORDS TO CHECK INTERVIEWER PERFORMANCE

Interviewers keep a call record for each attempt they make to identify and contact a subject. Figure 3.1 shows a call record from the Loma Prieta study. In this instance the designated respondent was particularly difficult to reach. The first call to the household was made at 5:35 p.m. on May 1, 1990. The interviewer conducted the screening interview (referred to as the *screener*) with the adult resident who answered the phone. The purpose of the screener in the Loma Prieta study was to find out whether the telephone number dialed was a residence, to determine who lived there, and whether adults in the household had also lived there on October 17, 1989, the date of the earthquake. The data collector listed all adult residents over 18, and then, using a Kish (1965) table, randomly selected a respondent from among them. The two rows of numbers in the upper right-hand corner of Figure 3.1 are a Kish table. The interviewer has circled the 2 in the top row and the 1 beneath it in the second row to indicate that there are 2 adults over 18 in this household who lived there on October 17, 1989, and that the first person listed on the household roster is the designated respondent.

Because the interviewer was speaking with the other adult during the screener, she now had to arrange to interview the designated respondent. The interviewer

38

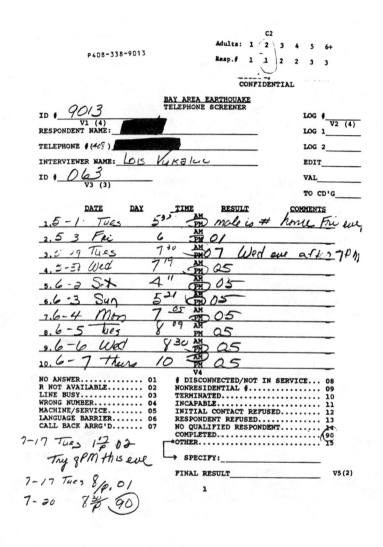

Figure 3.1. Using a Call Record to Monitor Interviewer Behavior

learned that the other adult was a male who would be home Friday evening. She called back on Friday evening, but there was no answer. On the following Tuesday evening she called again, and was told to call on Wednesday evening after 7:00 p.m. When she called on Wednesday, she got an answering machine. She then changed tactics and tried to contact the respondent on the weekend, but had no success. Periodically over the next week she made several more unsuccessful attempts to reach the targeted respondent. Then she gave up trying to reach him for a month, while she was busy interviewing others. Finally she reached and interviewed the respondent on Friday, July 20, at 8:30 p.m.

This call record documents the work of a conscientious interviewer. Notice how the interviewer persisted and called at different times of the day and on different days of the week. Obviously, attempts cannot go on forever. Usually, the number of callback attempts is determined by the research budget.

Call records provide a good one-page summary of an interviewer's work, particularly as it affects the makeup of the sample. While call records can be falsified, falsified records usually do not result in completed interviews. For example, in the Loma Prieta study, one new interviewer was given a list of 10 telephone numbers from the computer-generated list. A week later he returned 10 screeners to the office and reported that all 10 numbers did not exist, were disconnected, were businesses, or were for FAX machines. Because this was such an exceptionally low yield (generating zero out of a potential 10 interviews), the field supervisor called the numbers and found that the call records had been falsified. The interviewer was fired.

Call records are a valuable way to document and validate both personal interviews and off-site telephone interviews. When telephone interviews are conducted from a central location or computer-assisted telephone interviewing is used, there are more efficient ways to monitor data collectors' behavior and the status of the sample. CATI, for example, keeps track of whether a number was dialed and what the outcome was. Direct supervision can be used when calls are made from a central location.

Editing

Once data are collected, editing and data entry begin. Editing involves identifying and correcting errors that occur over the course of the study. Researchers must not forget to allow enough money for editing in their research budgets; the U.S. Office of Management and Budget (1990, p. 13) estimates that editing absorbs a minimum of 20% of the cost of most federal surveys.

Errors can occur in the design of data collection (see Chapter 2), because respondents intentionally or unintentionally make errors, because data collectors make errors, or during the creation of machine-readable files (see Chapter 4). Here we will describe how to identify and correct errors created by respondents and data collectors.

INTERVIEWER EDIT

The first stage of editing is done by the data collector or interviewer, who should carefully review each questionnaire as soon as possible after completion, while the interview is still fresh in mind. An *interviewer edit* ensures that handwriting is legible, no questions were missed, all skip instructions were followed, all information in boxes is coded, numbers corresponding to precoded answers have been circled, and all identifying information has been appropriately filled out.

When a questionnaire has open-ended questions or residual "other" categories for closed-ended questions, the interviewer must make sure that answers are filled out legibly and completely. During the interview, interviewers can reduce the likelihood of incomplete answers if they record *all* probes used to elicit responses and write down *everything* respondents say. Only when a subject says something like "I can't think of anything else" in response to the final probe: "What else can you tell me about [. . .]?" should the interviewer go on to the next question.

Sometimes the interviewer needs to clarify material so that supervisors or other office staff know data are correct. For example, if there is a discrepancy between the roster of persons living in the household and the number of persons reported as dependent upon household income, an interviewer needs to explain this or the supervisor might assume there is an error in the data. This situation occurred more than once in our earthquake studies. The "error" was explained by a note written by the interviewer stating that children were away at college or alimony was being paid to an ex-spouse.

If during this editing process an interviewer finds that answers to one or more questions are missing, he or she must call the respondent back immediately to obtain the missing data. Once the interviewer has completed the edit and made corrections, he or she returns the questionnaire or data form to the central office for logging-in and further editing.

LOGGING OR FIELD EDIT

The next edit is called the *logging* or *field edit*. Logging gives the researcher a quick assessment of how the data collectors are performing. Here supervisors make sure that the proper respondent was interviewed or the proper record was abstracted. They check the skip patterns to verify that they were followed correctly and review the call record sheet to ensure that it was completed properly. If errors are found, the questionnaire is returned to the interviewer for reinterview or correction. Similar checks are made if records are the source of data.

The field edit provides the major source of information about whether data collection is proceeding on schedule and whether the selected sample size is large enough to produce the necessary number of completed interviews. In every method of data collection, researchers must estimate the percentage of respondents or records that will result in usable, complete data records. If during the course of data collection supervisors note that the sample is not being obtained at the expected rate, decisions must be made quickly on how to change procedures or number of personnel to obtain the agreed-upon sample size. Failure to make such changes often extends data collection time, which leaves less time and money for data analysis and report writing.

During the *field edit* in our Whittier Narrows study, we discovered that our expectations about the number of subjects we needed were on the mark for most of Los Angeles County, but that we needed more telephone numbers to reach our goal of 200 interviews in the high-impact area. Consequently, an additional 274 telephone numbers were randomly generated. If we had not conducted the *field edit* we might not have known that our sample was seriously inadequate until we started analyzing our data.

QUALITY-CONTROL EDIT

The third edit is a *quality-control edit*. Here every item in the questionnaire or record abstraction form is checked for completeness, consistency, and clarity. When errors are found, the interview is referred back to the interviewer for clarification or reinterview. While the exact content of a quality-control edit varies for each research project, the following summarizes what should be included in a quality-control edit. Researchers must take each of the following steps:

1. Check household rosters to be sure they are correctly and fully filled out.
2. Check that data were collected from the correct record, respondent, household, or the like.
3. Evaluate all data submitted by data collectors to ensure their overall patterns of tallying responses and completion rates are in line with study expectations and respondent refusals are not significantly different from those of other data collectors.
4. Use call records to evaluate whether interviewers are varying their attempts to find respondents. Use similar methods to log and monitor data collection efforts of record abstractors and observers.
5. Resolve ambiguities in instrument use that can surface during data collection; for example, check that collectors explain disparities between the number of persons dependent on reported household income and the number of persons living in the household.
6. Check that missing data (e.g., don't know, inapplicable, refusal, missing) have been appropriately and consistently recorded.
7. Check whether precoded response categories for closed-ended questions are being used appropriately. If there are indications that problems exist,

this means that data collectors need further training or response categories need to be revised. Such revisions should be made quickly, even in the middle of a study.

8. Check that interviewers are following instructions and asking all specified probes for eliciting answers to open-ended questions. Similar procedures can be developed to monitor data gathering of observers and record abstractors.

9. Monitor mileage claims or telephone charges of data collectors. Such information can confirm or fail to support claims about work performed.

10. Record the time taken for data collection and evaluate significant deviations from it.

11. Be sensitive to data that are too perfect.

With the exceptions of items 10 and 11, all these points were discussed earlier in this chapter. Clearly, a data collector who consistently turns in questionnaires that are incomplete, inconsistent, and illegible, or who consistently obtains data from the wrong person or record, should be terminated. Similarly, interviewers who consistently obtain a high number of refusals should be terminated. Evidence that a data collector is much faster or slower than other data collectors also may be reason for evaluation and possible termination. Interviewers who complete interviews too quickly may not be giving respondents sufficient time to hear the questions or consider their answers.

The "perfect" data form also gives reason to pause. Human beings and the records they create are rarely completely consistent. When a data collector always turns in forms with no evidence of error on the part of the data collector or changes in responses by respondents, it is possible that the data collector "created" the data.

Similar kinds of problems may develop with self-administered questionnaires. Here the respondent, not the data collector, may be falsifying data. Respondents falsify data for many reasons; for instance, they may wish to present a more favorable image of themselves (e.g., by lowering age or raising income), they may not know or cannot accurately remember an item, or they may wish to please the interviewer or data collector. Whether the problem lies with the respondent or the data collector, the only way to determine whether such suspicions are valid is to ask a different data collector to reinterview the respondent or reabstract the record.

DATA ENTRY EDIT

The final manual edit is done as data are entered into the computer. This *data entry edit* serves as a check on the prior three edits, but some concerns are addressed here for the first time. For example, the respondents' descriptions of their jobs and workplaces are coded using the Census Bureau's *Alphabetical*

Index of Industries and Occupations. If these data need clarification, data collectors may be asked to recontact respondents; but obviously, as one gets further from the actual time of data collection, the ability to resolve problems declines and eventually data are lost.

Summary

While describing four stages of manual data editing, we have emphasized three points: Preliminary data editing should be done as close to the time of data collection as possible, to maximize the ability to make corrections while respondents and data sources are still available; data editing should include checks on the sample and its availability; and all data should be edited by more than one person. We suggest that, at minimum, the data collector, a supervisor, and a data entry worker should independently examine data for consistency, completeness, and clarity.

4. DATA ENTRY

Once data collection has been completed and checked, the process of data entry and cleaning starts. During data entry the verbal or numeric data collected using questionnaires, abstraction forms, or observations are entered into a computer, principally as numeric data "codes." These data codes (discussed in Chapter 2), together with labels and other attributes of the variables, constitute the data file. *Data entry* refers to the process of computerizing the data. Although other methods of data entry are briefly mentioned, only keyboard entry is considered in this chapter.

In the first section of this chapter we review how the evolution from punch cards to personal computers has changed the ways that computers are used in research studies. In the second section, we discuss the mechanics of computerizing the study data, beginning with definition of data file structure and variables, continuing with entry of the basic data values, and finishing with initial screening and cleanup necessary to ensure that the data are complete and correct. The last section discusses the training of data entry personnel.

Creating Computerized Data Files: Then and Now

One commonly thinks of statistical data analysis as the prime application for computers in research studies. Over the last two decades, however, changes in computers probably have had a greater effect on data entry than on statistical analysis. We will take a brief look at how such changes have created data processing advantages for the new computer-aided work patterns in contrast to the shortcomings of some old ways of thinking about data processing.

THE OLD WAY: BATCH PROCESSING

The Punch Card Legacy. Punch cards were developed for data processing long before electronic computers were invented. The key feature of punch cards was invariant positioning of data. Combinations of hole punches resulted in each card column representing a single alphanumeric character or digit. Thus one 80-column card could represent 80 consecutive characters or digits of data. Each variable was entered into a specific column or group of columns, creating what became known as *fixed-format* data. The early punch card systems placed a premium on simple, regular data formats and minimal input. Extra blanks, field-separator delimiters, and other syntactic aids to human readability frequently increased error problems with slow mechanical card readers.

The Early Computers. The early mainframe computers were big, finicky about operating environments, difficult to program, expensive to run, and difficult to maintain. A researcher took great care to prepare data and program instructions to minimize computer time, and jobs were fed to the computer as prepackaged "batches" by trained operators. In short, mainframe computer systems enforced an economy where computer resources were highly valued and rationed, and clerical resources for off-line data preparation were regarded as relatively cheap.

THE CONTEMPORARY WAY: COMPUTER-AIDED WORK

Beginning with the introduction of solid-state electronic components, the computer world changed radically. *Multiprocessing* and *time-sharing* capabilities allowed people to use the computers via *remote* keyboard terminals and display screens. Computers could now be used effectively to minimize overall production costs and to make things easier for workers who were not computer experts. Specifically, computers could be utilized to improve everyday error-prone human tasks such as data entry, as well as to perform difficult statistical computations.

The Desktop Personal Computer. The culmination (so far) of this revolution has come in the last decade. The desktop computer and the computer terminal connected to a midsize departmental computer are common office tools along with copiers, fax machines, and telephones. Workers routinely use spreadsheet, word-processing, and simple database programs for daily tasks. To take advantage of computer-aided work patterns, the developers of statistical analysis program packages have created data entry systems that use the PC in an interactive fashion, making data entry easier, quicker, and more accurate.

Expanding Horizons. Several advances suggest even easier times ahead for routine data entry operations. Computer-assisted interviewing techniques and scanners that read and enter documents directly into the computer will augment and, in some cases, replace keyboard entry of data. The increasing availability of mainframe-type relational database management systems on PCs will improve access to extensive bodies of data such as those needed by large, recurrent surveys. Perhaps most important for the PC user, the emergence of multitasking and windowing operating systems should speed up and ease the work of data entry, cleaning, and analysis.

We look next at the practical activities of defining data files, entering data, and cleaning out the errors.

Creating the Data File

Before data entry can begin (and ideally at the same time that data collection forms are designed), the researcher must decide how the data are to be organized. A data file can be simple—a few columns and rows of numbers—or an intricate collection of data values, definitions of variables, related data entry forms, and cleaning specifications. For a very small project, a researcher might opt to enter data into a table using a simple editing program. For a very large project or a continuing survey service, one may need an industrial-strength relational database management system augmented by custom editing features. We will cover the middle ground, concentrating on ways to create well-structured and documented data files of moderate size with standard data entry programs that are included in major statistical packages.

PACKAGE PROGRAMS FOR DATA ENTRY

One of the consequences of the broad acceptance of personal computers has been a proliferation of computer programs. We have chosen to illustrate our discussion with the data entry offerings from two major statistical program packages: SPSS Data Entry II (SPSS, 1987) and SAS FSP FSEDIT (SAS, 1987). In this chapter, we will refer to the data entry components simply as SPSS and SAS. BMDP, the third major statistical package we use in our data analysis illustrations, has a data entry product planned for release just prior to the appearance of this volume.

THE SHAPE OF THE FILE

Computerized data files can assume many forms; however, for most statistical analyses of study data, the appropriate form is a *rectangular* data file—essentially a table. Each horizontal line represents the data record for a specific case or subject, and each vertical field represents a particular variable for that case.

The variables are in the same order for each case. A rectangular data file is needed to run statistical packages such as SPSS, SAS, and BMDP, although the programs have some capability to change hierarchical files into rectangular ones.

Usually each *record* in a data file represents an individual case or person. The designation of what a record represents depends, however, on the *unit of analysis* for the study. If an individual person is the unit of analysis, then all the data for one person in the sample constitute one record in the data file. If the study is examining a sample of hospitals, school classrooms, or census tracts, then the unit of analysis is a hospital, a school classroom, or a census tract. (Sometimes a study has multiple units of analysis; for example, a household and each of the people in the household. In such studies, the researcher might set up multiple data sets or create hierarchical data sets. This book does not cover the alternative structures of complex files and problems associated with them.)

When we speak of a variable in rectangular data files or in tables, we are referring to a *field* of similar data items (age, for instance). A variable field may be as narrow as a single character, a group of digits, a dollar sign and decimal point for a money variable, or it may be an entire language phrase resulting from an open-ended question. Most numeric data items are converted to different forms in internal computer storage, not necessarily related to the printed width of the field. The implication, then, is that a rectangular file denotes a constant number of variable fields for successive cases or subjects (records) and not necessarily a constant number of punch card columns or bytes of computer memory space.

THE FORMAT AND CONTENTS OF THE DATA FILE

ASCII Files. The simplest type of data file has fields consisting of groups of digits or letters that are held in random-access memory (RAM) or stored on computer storage media (hard disks, floppy disks, tapes, and so on) in character image form as ASCII (American Standard Code for Information Interchange) character codes. (In mainframe computers another character coding, EBCDIC—for Extended Binary-Coded-Decimal Information Code—may be used.) The character image format does not have numeric digits converted into an internal binary form that is efficient for computation. Typically, file formats referred to as ASCII lack any data description information to define the types and names of variables, allowable value ranges, and so on. However, an ASCII file can be created and edited by any simple text editor program, is easily transportable from one program or computer to another, and is close to being a universal standard. Most of the common statistical packages, spreadsheet programs, word processors, and database managers can import and export ASCII file formats (often referred to as raw-data files). Sometimes ASCII files are referred to as DOS files on IBM-compatible PCs.

PC Spreadsheet and Database Files. Most research groups and PC users are familiar with spreadsheet programs such as Lotus 123 and database programs such as dBASE. These programs, therefore, are sometimes used for data entry, especially of small- to moderate-size study results. The data files created from these programs may include names for the fields (variables), format and field width information, and some coding of missing values. The regular file formats from these programs have in some cases become de facto standards for data interchange because of their widespread use, and the file formats of one program are often readable by the others.

The major statistical analysis programs make various provisions for input of data from these sources. For example, SPSS can read the regular files from several different spreadsheet and several database programs, taking in not only the raw data values for the variables but also variable names, data types, input field widths, and the like. SAS provides a means (DBF and DIF procedures) for converting back and forth between database and spreadsheet program formats and SAS data sets. BMDP does not accept input in the regular formats of spreadsheet, database, and word-processing programs, but suggests exporting ASCII (character image) output from those programs for input into BMDP. Variable names, types, and so on cannot be transferred directly.

Statistical Program System Files. The major statistical packages provide special versions of data files that encode additional information about the file along with the data values. In SPSS, for example, a *system file* contains the data items in internal binary format specific to the computer in use, a dictionary containing definitions of the variables, and even data entry forms, cleaning specifications, and skip values. In BMDP a somewhat comparable internal file format is known as a *BMDP file*, and in SAS as a *SAS data set*. These specialized files, the *SPSS system file*, for example, provide several advantages. They keep all of the related information, such as variable names, with the basic data so that it need not be entered again for successive statistical analyses. Such files provide the investigators with much of the information needed for a codebook of the data as described in Chapter 6. They also facilitate the use of the files by a number of investigators, since the documentation for the data is on-line. Furthermore, they keep the numeric data in an internal binary format for computational efficiency, whereby speed of computation is enhanced. Finally, they provide an easy way to enhance the data file with newly added derived variables, identification of missing values, transformations, and additional labels to be used in subsequent analyses.

Unfortunately, the formats and information included are unique to each of the proprietary statistical analysis program systems—that is, all of the information in an SPSS system file is not *directly* usable in BMDP or SAS programs, and so on. However, the major program systems provide some mechanisms for reading each other's files. For example, on mainframe computers, SAS release 6 can read SPSS and SPSS-X files, but, as of this writing, SPSS cannot read SAS release 6 files. SPSS can, however, read SAS release 5 files, which SAS release 6 has the capability of creating. DBMS/COPY provides for transfers on PCs. The ability to move from program to program may change in future versions; readers are advised to check with their local computer facilities.

Because the data are stored in a hardware-dependent binary format, it is not usually possible to use a system file from one type of computer in another. A BMDP file created on a PC will not be directly usable on a VAX or an IBM mainframe computer. The BMDP and SPSS statistical program systems provide for *portable* versions of their system files for export and import between different computer hardware systems, and for transfer between mainframes and PCs. SAS also has provisions for preparing programs and data files that can be used with SAS on different computers.

Major computer centers often have utilities that help in exchanging data between program system files. Software is available for PCs to accomplish many file transfers (for example, a commercially available program, DBMS/COPY, will transfer files among a wide selection of spreadsheets, database programs, and statistical packages), and books are available that discuss file formats and transfers (for example, see Poor, 1990). Nonetheless, the simplest procedure is to enter the data using a data entry package that is part of the statistical program system you intend to use.

DEFINING THE DATA FILE

In using the structured data entry programs (as provided in the major statistical packages), one begins by naming the file and then defining the variables. These defined variables are then used in the program to guide data entry operations. Using SPSS, for example, one starts with the *Files Branch* to name a data file, then uses the *Dictionary Branch* to define the variables to be included in the file. The definition of each variable is done in an entry window, as illustrated below, that prompts for the variable attributes. The attributes in the left column prompt the user by showing the kind of information that can be described during data entry. The middle column provides an example of information that a user might enter, while the right column in the illustration describes the options that are available for each attribute.

Attribute	*Example*	*Description*
Variable Name	**marital**	(up to eight characters)
Variable Label	**marital status**	(up to 60 characters)
Type of Variable	**numeric**	(**numeric** or **string**)
Variable Length	**1**	(max for input/display)
Decimal Places	**0**	(number, for display)
Display Mode	**edit**	(**edit**, **verify**, or **display**)
Missing	**9**	(up to three codes)

SPSS allows one to assign labels to specified values of a variable. For example, for the variable *marital*:

Value	Label
1	**never married**
2	**married**
3	**formerly married**
9	**missing**

When variables have been defined in this fashion, the data file is permanently documented in computer-readable form. These variable definitions are then available to guide data entry, to facilitate cleaning of the data file, to provide necessary information for statistical analysis, and to annotate displays and printouts of results. The various data entry programs handle null or missing values differently. Refer to the system manuals for detailed provisions for defaults and missing value codes.

Figure 4.1 shows a frequency distribution from the Whittier Narrows study computed using the SPSS statistical analysis programs, with and without variable and missing value labels. To understand and interpret the table in part A of this figure, the researcher would have to refer to a codebook or questionnaire. In contrast, the table in part B can be understood and interpreted directly. Here, the variable label indicates that this is the frequency distribution for Question 50, which asks about ethnicity. The value labels identify the various codes or categories of ethnicity. Although it is tedious to create variable and value labels, their existence saves a great deal of time during analysis. They also provide partial documentation for a data set. Thus we recommend that when such a capability exists, variable labels and value labels be created for *all* data.

The SAS data entry procedure uses operations generally comparable to those of SPSS for definition of data files and their variables, although the details and the particular variable attributes used differ. For instance, SAS allows specifying of maximum and minimum allowable values for a variable as part of the variable definition, while SPSS obtains this information as part of *cleaning specifications*.

ENTERING THE DATA

The contemporary concept of computer-aided work is evident in data entry operations. Using SPSS, for example (or SAS data entry equivalents), the user does not need to keep track constantly of the order of variables, the number of characters in a data field, or the number of decimal places to enter for a value. The next variable for which a value is to be entered is clearly highlighted on the display screen, and many common input errors will be detected and rejected by the computer program, which indicates that correction is needed. The major advance is that the user no longer needs to know, or care, about inconsequential detail in data entry. Whether

A. Variable Without Labels
   V547

VALUE LABEL	VALUE	FREQUENCY	PERCENT	VALID PERCENT	CUM PERCENT
	1	563	81.6	81.6	81.6
	2	62	9.0	9.0	90.6
	3	46	6.7	6.7	97.2
	4	4	.6	.6	97.8
	5	13	1.9	1.9	99.7
	7	2	.3	.3	100.0
	TOTAL	690	100.0	100.0	

VALID CASES   690   MISSING CASES   0

B. Variable With Labels
   V547   Q50-ETHNICITY

VALUE LABEL	VALUE	FREQUENCY	PERCENT	VALID PERCENT	CUM PERCENT
WHITE	1	563	81.6	83.4	
BLACK	2	62	9.0	9.2	92.6
ASIAN	3	46	6.7	6.8	99.4
NAT AMER	4	4	.6	.6	100.0
OTHER	5	13	1.9	MISSING	
REFUSED	7	2	.3	MISSING	
	TOTAL	690	100.0	100.0	

VALID CASES   675   MISSING CASES   15

Figure 4.1. Variable With and Without Variable Label and Value Labels

numeric values are right-justified, with leading zeros rather than blanks, is no longer a concern of the user; the program has accepted the significant value typed in, and properly incorporated it into the developing internal data file structure.

One example will help to illustrate this shift in functions between human operator and computer. In the past, when developing a coding frame (see Chapter 2), one might have agonized over whether to allow two digits or three for a variable code for a postcoded open-end response. If the computer is keeping track and incorporating the input data into one of the *system file* formats as entered, this concern is unnecessary. The internal binary format for the numeric value occupies the same amount of storage (typically 8 bytes) whether the code is 2, 3, or 15 digits.

Researchers have often avoided using shortcut techniques such as free-format input with field separators (comma or blank delimiters), elimination of nonsignificant leading zeros, and null entries for skipped variables. Their rationale has been that conversion of this abridged data entry information back into fully detailed fixed-format records would involve esoteric computer programming work or be fraught with error opportunities, and that visual proofing of the data as entered is error prone. The advantage of the contemporary data entry packages is that the data can be displayed or printed for user proofing at any stage in the operation—before and after cleaning, after range checking or transformations—in exactly the format used during input.

FORMS OR SPREADSHEETS?

The data entry programs discussed here allow alternative formats for data entry: a one-record-at-a-time mode generally known as a *form*, and a *spreadsheet* or *table* mode that directly represents the rectangular data file being created. SPSS allows instant switching back and forth between the modes. (With SAS the process of switching is somewhat less immediate, as the form and spreadsheet modes are implemented with different programs.)

The choice between these modes is in part a matter of personal preference, but the shape and size of the data file should be considered in the choice.

Spreadsheet. A tabular format for data entry where rows represent cases or records and columns represent variables is often called a spreadsheet. The spreadsheet entry mode requires no special setup and is efficient for small data files. The ability to see the input from previous records while entering new data can be helpful. If a data file has relatively few variables, scrolling left and right will not be required to view them all on the display screen in the spreadsheet mode.

Figure 4.2 presents an abbreviated example of spreadsheet data for three cases and seven variables using the questions given in Figure 2.2. Fields to the left of V92 or to the right of V97 are seen by scrolling the spreadsheet left or right on the computer display screen. Respondents with IDs 8002 and 2453 answered yes (coded 1) to V92 (Question 1), and the next four variables were skipped and coded 0 for "not applicable." ID 8910 answered no (coded 2) to V92 (Question 1) and, therefore, was asked Questions 1A-1C, which resulted in codes for V93-V96, and was then skipped past V97 (Question 2) to Question 8. V97 (Question 2) was coded 0 for "not applicable."

Form. The *form* mode uses the whole computer screen for the current case being entered. There are several arguments for using the *form* mode of input:

- An entry form can be structured to look like the original data collection instrument.
- Variables do not have to be entered in the order in which they were defined, if another entry order is useful.
- Large numbers of variables for each record can be accommodated easily with multiple-page forms. Flipping pages on the display typically is an easier and faster operation than scrolling a display left and right.

ID	...	V92 Q1	V93 Q1A	V94 Q1B	(V95 Q1C	V96) Q1C	V97 Q2	...

Variable and Question No.

ID	...	V92 Q1	V93 Q1A	V94 Q1B	(V95 Q1C	V96) Q1C	V97 Q2	...
8002 ...		1	0	0	0	0	1	...
.				→ skip ——————————				
.								
.								
2453 ...		1	0	0	0	0	2	...
.				→ skip ——————————				
.								
.								
8910 ...		2	5	19	1	0	0	...
.						→ skip to Q8		
.								
.								

Figure 4.2. Example of Data Entry Spreadsheet Using Questions From Figure 2.2

- Long variables (such as from direct text entry of open-ended question responses) can be accommodated easily.
- Short coding comments and instructions can be included on the screen as prompts for the user.

Figure 4.3 presents an example of forms input using the first case from Figure 4.2. The information displayed on the screen corresponds to the data collection documents being read, with abbreviated text and code values, and explanatory notes or entry instructions added. The form may contain many pages (screens) to accommodate all of the variables for the data file, but the data entered on a set of pages represents a single case or respondent—equivalent to a single line on the spreadsheet in Figure 4.2. Here the data shown represent the respondent with ID 8002, also shown in Figure 4.2.

The two major statistical packages discussed in this chapter differ in how they implement *forms*. SPSS provides the features described here, tailored especially to the entry of survey and other research data. SAS provides similar features while allowing more options, but with more complexity.

SKIP-AND-FILL OPERATIONS IN DATA ENTRY

Particularly in survey studies, it is common to have branching sequences of variables in a data file (see Chapter 2). Given one response to a question, a more detailed sequence of follow-up questions is asked; otherwise, the detailed

53

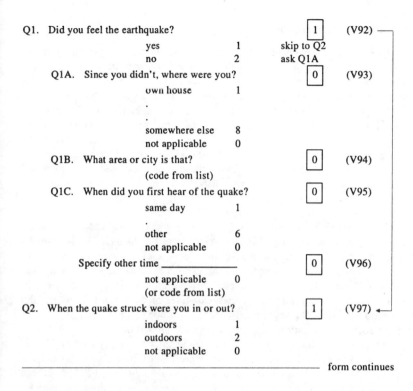

Figure 4.3. Example of a Data Entry Form Using Questions From Figure 2.2 With Data From Respondent 8002

sequence is skipped or an alternative sequence is pursued. At coding or data entry time the unasked questions need to be addressed, usually coded as "not applicable." The major statistical package data entry programs can be utilized in several ways to streamline handling of these skip-and-fill operations.

SPSS provides full support for skip-and-fill operations. For example, the entry of a particular predetermined code (e.g., 1 for yes) as the response to a variable causes the computer to move automatically to the first of a sequence of follow-up variables for entry. Entering a different response to the same question causes the program to skip over the follow-up variables and automatically enter predefined "not applicable" codes for them. SAS does not explicitly provide full support for skip-and-fill operations, but the user can approximate this capability through a series of programming operations.

CLEANING THE DATA FILE

Once the data set has been created, it must be cleaned. During cleaning, errors that occurred during data entry or that were not found prior to data entry are identified and corrected. The researcher checks the data for values that are out of range and for errors that show up as inconsistencies between variables.

Cleaning a data file involves a variety of checks. On small data files, many of these checks can be performed informally by a visual scan of a printout from the file, but for files with many records, many variables, skip-and-fill branching, or long string variables for open-ended text responses, a visual check is unproductive.

Range checking, checking variable values against predefined maximum and minimum bounds, is often done as a data screening or cleaning technique to catch spurious values or keyboard entry errors; for example, if 100 has been entered instead of 10.

SPSS provides for *cleaning specifications* that can be invoked *either* during data entry or, later, as a separate cleaning process for the data file. In addition to the range or bounds checking described above, cleaning rules can be formulated that are logical expressions making various assertions about the data (see Chapter 5). The cleaning process tests these assertions against each record in turn and produces a report that shows violations of the rules. SAS allows the definition of valid data ranges as part of the definition of variables, and provides an interactive error indication during keyboard input of data.

Comparable cleaning operations can be done after data entry with any statistical package program by running univariate statistical programs or procedures in which logical expressions (the cleaning rules) are applied to the data records as a *transformation* operation in which records with violations are thereby flagged for editing (see Chapter 5).

Consistency Checks Using Contingency Tables. Even when data appear clean following range checks, consistency checks may reveal errors. Part A of Figure 4.4 shows a cross-tabular table of two variables from Figure 2.2: V98 (Question 2A), "Where were you when the earthquake struck?" by V92 (Question 1), "Did you feel the earthquake?" (V92 and V98 are the variable names assigned when the data file was defined.)

Remember that this series of questions is in skip-and-fill format. A person who said yes to Question 1 (V92) *should* have been asked Question 2A (V98); a person who said no to Question 1 *should not* have been asked Question 2A. Thus there is something wrong with the data entered for the 5 respondents who are coded 1 on V92 and 0 on V98 and for the 7 respondents who are coded 2 on V92 and 1, 3, 4, or 7 on V98. We track down this problem by finding the identification numbers of these 12 cases, looking up their answers in the questionnaires, and correcting the computer file. Part B of Figure 4.4 shows the contingency table between the two variables after all the corrections were made.

A. Contingency Table Showing Inconsistencies

V92 COUNT	V98 NOT APP 0	OWN HOME 1	OTH HOME 2	WORK 3	SCHOOL 4	TRAV-ELING 5	PUB PLACE 6	OTHER 7	ROW TOTAL
YES 1	5	416	7	114	9	51	1	20	623 90.3
NO 2	60	3		2	1			1	67 9.7
COLUMN TOTAL	65 9.4	419 60.7	7 1.0	116 16.8	10 1.4	51 7.4	1 .1	21 3.0	690 100.0

NUMBER OF MISSING OBSERVATIONS = 0

B. Contingency Table Showing Corrected Inconsistencies

V92 COUNT	V98 NOT APP 0	OWN HOME 1	OTH HOME 2	WORK 3	SCHOOL 4	TRAV-ELING 5	PUB PLACE 6	OTHER 7	ROW TOTAL
YES 1		420	7	114	9	52	1	20	623 90.3
NO 2	67								67 9.7
COLUMN TOTAL	67 9.7	420 60.9	7 1.0	114 16.5	9 1.3	52 7.5	1 .1	20 2.9	690 100.0

NUMBER OF MISSING OBSERVATIONS = 0

Figure 4.4. Contingency Tables to Diagnose Inconsistencies Between Question 1 and Question 2A From Figure 2.2

Timing of Data Cleaning. The entire data set should be cleaned prior to analyzing any of the data. All too frequently, no effort is made to clean data, or data are cleaned in a piecemeal fashion as errors are discovered. Range checks can be done during data entry, or after data entry by running frequency distributions of all the variables in the data set. Errors usually can be spotted quite easily and, as we saw in part B of Figure 4.1, the addition of value labels for legitimate codes helps make illegal codes "pop out" in a frequency distribution. Consistency checks are more difficult to conduct, and it is more difficult to know exactly when to stop making them.

Cleaning of Longitudinal Data Sets. In some studies data collection occurs at multiple times over a period of months or years. Data cleaning in such studies is more complicated, and it is important to do it as soon as possible after each wave of data collection. It is particularly important to check demographic information or other information that should remain constant or change in predictable directions over time. For example, the respondent's gender, age, education, occupation, ethnicity, and number of children should either stay constant or change consistently over time.

There are, of course, situations in which legitimate changes do occur or reporting errors are made by the respondent. Respondents often forget about children who are away at college or in the military, sometimes falsify their own ages, and change their occupations or ethnic identities. Such cases are rare, however, and when these inconsistencies occur they must be checked and the discrepancy corrected, the data declared missing, the case dropped, or the reason for the discrepancy documented.

HOW CLEAN IS CLEAN?

Determining that the data file contains no out-of-range or inconsistent values does not mean that it contains no errors. An incorrect keystroke can result in a numeric value that is in the accepted range and for which no logical inconsistency exists. If a level of close-to-zero errors is desired, reentering the entire data file and comparing the results can be considered. The SPSS data entry program includes a "verify" mode in which the data being entered the second time are compared with those entered the first time. If the two values disagree, both values are displayed so that the data entry person can decide which to use. Alternatively, the data can be entered twice as if they were additional variables for each case. The order of entry of the cases should be identical. The resulting data set will have the same number of cases but twice the number of variables. Then, the first half of the variables are subtracted from the second half and any nonzero results are checked. Note that if the values entered the second time are identical to the first entry, all the differences should be zero. Obviously, the confidence in the data will be much greater if the data are verified, particularly for large data sets entered by unmotivated staff. It will double the cost of data entry, however, so careful assessment should be made of the extra cost versus the benefits of error-free data entry.

Training of Data Entry Personnel

Like data collectors, coders and data entry clerks must be trained and supervised. This is particularly important if coders and data entry clerks are hired only for those tasks. Such work tends to be repetitive and tedious, and it demands attention to detail. Persons who have no understanding of or interest in the outcome of the study frequently do not understand why accuracy and consistency are important in coding and data entry. We have found that full-time data entry personnel tend to make fewer entry errors than research assistants.

Many of the procedures used with data collectors can be modified for use in hiring, training, and supervising data processing personnel. Procedures to be used in coding and entering data should be reviewed in sequence and in detail. The researcher should have each person code and enter two or three "practice" forms. The practice forms should be selected or created to represent the kinds of problems expected during data entry.

Once actual coding and data entry begin, at least 10-25% of the work should be reviewed for accuracy. This can be done by use of available computer verification programs (e.g., SPSS and BMDP), by personal review of the work of individual data processors, or by having two data processors independently code or enter the same data and comparing their results. Any discrepancies must be examined and resolved. Data entry that involves a complex sequence of actions or that requires data processors to make judgment decisions should be monitored more frequently. In general, the coding and data entry associated with open-ended questions is more difficult than that associated with closed-ended questions. In large data sets with complex coding or data entry problems, it is sometimes advantageous to have a single person "specialize" in coding or entering certain kinds of data. Examples might include the use of the International Classification of Diseases to code information from hospital records or the use of the U.S. Census Bureau's (1992) *Alphabetical Index of Industries and Occupations* to code occupational status.

Even after careful instructions on the part of the researcher, problems surface during coding and data entry that are not anticipated. Coders and data entry clerks should be encouraged to watch for problems and to bring them to the attention of the researcher. If a problem is widespread or important, coding and data entry procedures should be modified and data already entered must be reviewed and, if necessary, corrected.

5. DATA PREPARATION FOR ANALYSIS

Once the data have been entered into the computer and a complete and documented data file is obtained, the data must be processed prior to analysis. For small data sets, data processing can be performed concurrently with statistical analysis, but for larger studies, it should be performed as a separate step. In the separate step, a data file of usable documented data is created that all the investigators on the project can analyze directly. This simplifies the entry of statistical instructions, because all the data processing steps are already completed.

One of the first steps in data processing (sometimes called data management) is to determine the *response* rate for the study and to decide if the sample

58

obtained reflects the population from which it was taken. Subsequent steps include *data screening* for incomplete or missing data, possible *data imputation* for missing values, *outlier detection*, *transformations* to create more easily analyzed variables, *scale* evaluation, and *saving* the results in one or more working files and subfiles. The various computer program packages use similar data management methods, but the actual instructions vary. Here we discuss the methods, but do not give specific computer instructions; these can be obtained from the appropriate manuals. We assume that the reader has options equivalent to those found in SPSS, SAS, or BMDP program packages. To start the process, run a univariate statistical program such as EXAMINE or FREQUENCIES in SPSS, UNIVARIATE in SAS, or 2D in BMDP to obtain a simple data description on all the variables. This will list the number of missing values per variable, the maximum and minimum values for each variable, the number of responses in each category for nominal or ordinal variables, and summary statistics such as means, medians, and standard deviations.

Nonresponse

Data may be unavailable for two reasons (see Kalton & Kasprzyk, 1986). The first occurs when no information is available on a subject either because of refusal or because the subject (or the subject's record) cannot be found. We call this *nonresponse*. The second occurs when partial data are available from the subject but some items are missing. We call this *missing data*.

If there is appreciable nonresponse, investigators should attempt to evaluate how subjects with no data compare with subjects for whom data exist. One common check is to compare the demographic characteristics of the sample (age, gender, and so on) with those of the population from which it came. If the gender and age distribution of the population is known, the comparison is simple. If not, then census or other data thought to characterize the population are used. If it is determined that the sample obtained is not representative of the population, the magnitude of the difference should be assessed. For example, in survey samples women are often overrepresented. Typically, such discrepancies are simply reported, but the data from underrepresented groups (e.g., men) can also be weighted more in the analyses to approximate their representation in the population.

USE OF WEIGHTS

Weighting may be particularly important if results are to be used in projecting the need for services such as school or medical care. For example, if a community is considering building or relocating schools, projections as to the number, geographic location, and age distribution of children expected to attend school in the community must be as accurate as possible. In such cases, distributions on important variables in the sample should reflect the population, and the following formula for weighted sample means should be used (see Kalton & Kasprzyk, 1986, for an estimate of the bias of the unadjusted mean):

$$\bar{y}(w) = \sum W(j)\bar{y}(j)$$

where $W(j)$ denotes the proportion of the population in stratum j, $\bar{y}(j)$ denotes the mean of the subjects in stratum j in the sample, and $\bar{y}(w)$ denotes the overall weighted mean. This formula assumes that a simple random sample has been drawn. For further discussion, see Kish (1965) or Little and Rubin (1987). The major statistical packages allow for the use of weights.

Typically, the sample is divided into groups or strata using the variables (gender, age, and so on) on which response is anticipated to be dissimilar. The number of respondents and nonrespondents within each stratum is computed. Weights are computed proportional to the inverse of the response rate within each stratum (see Kalton & Kasprzyk, 1986). For example, suppose you obtained the following response by gender:

	Respondents	Nonrespondents	Sum
Male	100	60	160
Female	150	10	160
Sum	250	70	320

The response rate for males would be $100/160 = 0.6250$, and for females $150/160 = 0.9375$. The weights could be taken as $1/.625$ or 1.60 for males and 1.0667 for females, or could be adjusted further so that the sum of the weights equals the sample size. The adjusted weights are computed as

$$W(i) = w(i) \times N(r)/N(t)$$

where $w(i)$ is the original weight in the ith weighting stratum, $N(r)$ is the total sample size of responders, and $N(t)$ is the number of responders and nonresponders. For males, we would have

$$1.60 \times 250/320 = 1.25$$

and for females 0.833. Since we have 100 males and 150 females in the sample, the sum of the weights is

$$100 \times 1.25 + 150 \times 0.833 = 250$$

(the sample size).

Logistic regression analysis provides another method of estimating weights. The existence or nonexistence of a response is treated as a dichotomous dependent variable and other variables are used to predict it (see Afifi & Clark, 1990; Hosmer & Lemeshow, 1989). If, for example, you have information on age, education, and gender *and* you can predict whether or not a person responded using these three variables, your respondents and nonrespondents differ on these characteristics. Logistic regression provides you with an estimate of the probability that a given subject's data will be missing. These probabilities can then be assigned as weights for all cases; cases that have missing data are given higher weights.

It has been our experience that the use of weights does not substantially change estimates of the sample mean unless nonrespondents are appreciably different from respondents and there is a substantial proportion of nonrespondents. Note that the use of significance tests with weighted data sets is not straightforward unless the weights are known to be without error.

Missing Data

For the second type of missing values, some data are available for all the subjects, but for certain subjects some data are missing. Such missing data will often be denoted in the computer files by a period or other symbol. Sometimes investigators distinguish among the different types of missing values, using responses such as "not applicable," "refused," "don't know," and "missing" (see Chapter 2).

All data sets should be examined for patterns of missing values. A small data set can be printed out and both *cases* and *variables* can be scanned for excessive missing values. If a subject has many missing values, the simplest procedure is to eliminate this case from the data set. The researcher may want to check the demographic characteristics of such subjects to see if there is something special about them. Variables (other than those legitimately skipped as "not applicable") that have many missing values probably should be eliminated. The objective is to reduce missing values to a minimum, scattered throughout rather than clustered in a few cases or variables.

When the data set is large, visual scanning is difficult and indirect methods of determining the patterns of missing values should be used. The major statistical packages can provide counts of the number of missing values by variable. SPSS and SAS allow you to rotate your data set so the variables become the cases and the cases the variables. You can then analyze the number of missing values per case. The BMDP AM program denotes missing values with an "M" and prints out the values that are either too small or too big; numerical values that are both present and within range are blank. This allows patterns of missing data to be discerned visually by scanning even quite large data sets. BMDP AM also provides the number of cases present by variable and by pairs of variables.

CASEWISE AND PAIRWISE DELETION OF CASES

Most statistical package programs allow multivariate analytical procedures to be done using either casewise or pairwise deletion of cases (see BMDP 8D or SPSS). Whenever possible, casewise (sometimes called listwise) deletion of cases is preferred. When casewise deletion of cases is used, only those cases that have data on *all* variables included in the analysis remain in the analysis. For example, if correlations were being computed between all pairs of five variables, only those cases with *no* missing data on *any* of the five variables would be included in the correlation matrix. This can result in an appreciable loss of cases if many variables are used. Suppose you wish to run a stepwise regression analysis that includes 25 variables. If 2% of the responses for each variable are missing completely at random, you will lose about 40% of your cases from the regression analysis.

When pairwise deletion of cases is used, the missing data for each pair of variables is examined. For example, if correlations were being computed between all pairs of five variables, the computer would be instructed to examine each unique pair. That is, if 100 cases in the study have no missing values on variables 1 and 2, those 100 cases are used to compute the correlation between variables 1 and 2. If, in contrast, 121 cases have no missing values on variables 1 and 3, those 121 cases are used in calculating the correlation between variables 1 and 3. As a result, each correlation coefficient conceivably could be calculated using a different sample size. With pairwise deletion, the typical correlation coefficient in a correlation matrix will be computed from a larger sample size than for casewise deletion. We recommend using this option *only if* the sample size is so small that it is critical to use all possible observations and the missing observations are missing at random, as discussed in the next section.

FILLING IN MISSING VALUES

In some instances you can go back to the individual subject or record and obtain information that fills in a missing value. This is recommended whenever feasible. Usually it is not possible, so you must either leave the value missing or fill it in using a procedure called *imputation*. Imputation procedures may be generally applicable to a variety of data or quite specific to a particular study. For example, in Chapter 2 we showed how an error in a "skip-and-fill" in the Whittier Narrows study resulted in some respondents not being asked for dollar estimates of the damage they experienced. These missing data were imputed by searching the data files for other subjects with similar types of damage, calculating the average amount of damage reported, and assigning the average to those for whom it was missing.

Before imputation is used, certain assumptions must be made about *how* the data are missing (Little & Rubin, 1987, 1990). Data can be missing completely at random (MCAR), missing at random (MAR), or nonrandomly missing. When data are MCAR, the missing values are randomly distributed across all cases. For example, if one page of the data collection instrument was missing, answers for that page might not be obtained for one case. When data are MCAR, cases with missing values are assumed to be like cases with no missing values. This can be checked by dividing subjects into two groups according to whether or not they have missing data. Characteristics of the two groups can then be compared using procedures such as t tests that test for equal means across the two groups (see BMDP 8D). If data are MCAR, no appreciable differences should be found between the two groups on any of the characteristics tested.

More complex multivariate analyses can also be performed. For categorical data (nominal or ordinal), chi-square or log linear analysis can be used. If the sample size is small, these tests may have low power. Also, in performing such tests it is important to consider what variables are likely to be different between the two groups and not to perform tests on all possible variables or combinations of variables. For example, if a question was worded in a complicated manner or assumed sophisticated knowledge, nonresponse might be expected to vary inversely with subjects' education. In such a case the mean education of responders and nonresponders should be compared.

When data are MCAR, several imputation techniques can be used to replace the missing values. The simplest is to replace the missing value with the variable mean derived from all the cases that were not missing. This technique is used when no other variable is known to be highly correlated with the missing variable. For example, suppose your data included heights of children and some of the heights were missing. You could use the mean height of the other children (called mean substitution) as an estimate of the missing height, but your estimate would be improved by first fitting a regression equation where the dependent or outcome variable was height and the independent or predictor variables were age and gender. The data from the children with no missing values would be used to compute the coefficients for the equation. Once the equation was computed, it would be used to predict the heights of the children with missing values by combining their age and gender with the coefficients obtained from the equation. These predicted heights would then be entered into the data set. This would lead to less biased results than mean substitution. Using mean substitution or a regression equation to predict an imputed height is called a *deterministic* method.

One problem with the regression substitution technique described above is that everyone with the same age and gender who has missing data is assigned exactly the same height. In the above example, a height of 50 inches might be assigned to all 10-year-old girls whose height was missing in the data set when, in fact, the heights of 10-year-old girls with no missing data vary around 50 inches. This will also result in the variance of the dependent variable being underestimated. In recognition of this problem, some researchers add a residual value to the predicted value obtained from the regression equation. The added residual can be obtained by using a residual from a randomly selected complete case or by sampling from a theoretical distribution of residuals (see Kalton & Kasprzyk, 1986, for further information). When residuals are used, the method is called *stochastic substitution*. The objective is to obtain imputed values that are similar to those for children without missing data. This stochastic method can also be used with mean substitution. (For other methods of imputation, see Anderson, Basilevsky, & Hum, 1983; Little & Rubin, 1987.)

Generally, missing data are not randomly distributed across all respondents but may be missing at random within one or more subgroups. For example, male respondents may have more missing data, but within the group of male respondents, those with missing data do not differ from those who answered the question. Values can be imputed when the missing data are MAR, but the procedures used are more complicated. One such procedure is "hot deck" imputation, in which the answer given by an individual who did respond and who is similar to the respondent in other characteristics is substituted for the missing value (see David, Little, Samuhel, & Triest, 1986; Ford, 1983). Another method is maximum likelihood estimation (see Little & Rubin, 1990). The BMDP AM program can be used to obtain maximum likelihood estimates.

Finally, the missing values may not meet the assumptions of being missing at random. When data are missing because of refusals or don't knows, this rarely occurs randomly across the entire sample or within an identifiable subgroup. In such cases, it is difficult to make a theoretical case for imputation, though there are times when imputation is practical nevertheless. For example, when responses to only one or two items are missing in a scale that contains numerous items, we recommend imputing the values for these items. Techniques for imputation in scales will be discussed later in this chapter.

IMPLICATIONS FOR ANALYSIS

In general, most researchers do not perform imputation. It involves a considerable amount of time, and some journal reviewers distrust one or more of the procedures used. One reason for this distrust is that analyses of the combined imputed and actual data treat the imputed values as if they were actual data and tend to provide too optimistic estimates of the significance levels. If the true level is, say, 10%, the level including imputed values may come out to be 5%. Statistics are biased once missing values are replaced, although the extent of the bias may be minor if very little is replaced. For example, when mean substitution is used, the variance is underestimated unless a residual term is added. On the other hand, unless data are MCAR, serious biases can occur if data analyses are limited to only those cases with complete data, and large reductions in sample size may lead to serious reductions in the power of statistical tests.

The statistical packages offer options that make replacement of particular missing values with means or other values straightforward, as, for example, BMDP AM as noted above and SPSS for mean substitution.

In some studies it may be important to analyze data both with and without the missing values replaced, and then compare the results to make sure that the method of replacing missing values did not lead to appreciably different interpretations. Other analyses can be performed that highlight the effect of cases with missing values. For example, the researcher can create a 0,1 dummy variable that reflects whether each case does (1) or does not (0) have information on important predictor variables. This dummy variable can be considered a predictor variable. Other predictor variables for which complete data exist can also be chosen. Finally, new, interactive predictor variables can be created using statistical package programs. These interactive variables are obtained by multiplying the dummy variable by each of the predictor variables for which complete data exist. (For an example of creating an interaction variable, see Afifi & Clark, 1990, p. 232.) The resultant regression equation contains three kinds of predictor variables: the predictor variables for which complete data exist, the dummy variable denoting cases for which an important predictor variable is missing, and all interactions between the dummy variable and the predictor variables with complete data. The dependent variable used should be an important dependent variable for which no cases are missing. In essence, this amounts to testing whether there are significant interaction coefficients between group status (i.e., missing versus nonmissing) and the effects of the predictor variables on the dependent variable. If all the interaction coefficients are insignificant predictors of the dependent variable, it is argued that one can, with some confidence, generalize from the equation computed from the sample with the complete data to the population from which the sample was drawn. (We want to thank an anonymous reviewer for this suggestion.)

Outliers

Outliers are observations that appear inconsistent with the rest of the data set (see Barnett & Lewis, 1984). Outliers can be avoided to a large extent by using range checks in data entry programs (see Chapter 4) or can be identified by running a univariate statistical package program and checking results against acceptable values. If the values obtained appear unreasonable, the distribution of observations for the variable should be examined. When variables are nominal (categorical) or ordinal (ordered data), the process of checking univariate distributions against acceptable values is usually sufficient to identify outliers. The decision that an interval variable contains outliers is more complicated. In this section the detection of outliers for interval or ratio data is discussed.

Three methods are commonly used for identifying outliers. First, researchers rely on their knowledge of the variable under study and declare an observation an outlier if it is outside the range of common experience. For example, most physicians would question a systolic blood pressure of 400 or an age of 128. Second, many researchers declare an observation an outlier if it appears to them to be far removed from the rest of the data set. Suppose you had the following data set: 1, 2, 3, 4, 5, 7, 8, and 25. The 25 is "unlike" the other observations in order of magnitude. This kind of outlier often can be detected by examining the percentile distributions available from many univariate summary programs. Finally, there are formal statistical tests for outliers (see Barnett & Lewis, 1984; Dunn & Clark, 1987; Hoaglin, Mosteller, & Tukey, 1983). The formal tests generally assume that variables are normally distributed, and are quite sensitive to lack of normality.

Outlier detection has received a great deal of attention, particularly in the context of regression analysis. As a result, many statistical packages include almost too many statistics (see Afifi & Clark, 1990; Chatterjee & Hadi, 1988; Cook & Weisberg, 1982). Chatterjee and Hadi (1988) include a chapter on detection of multiple outliers, and Rousseeuw and van Zomeren (1990) discuss methods of detecting multiple outliers in multivariate point clouds.

When an observation is clearly an outlier and seems quite unreasonable, most researchers have little hesitation in deleting it. The ones that are difficult to decide on are those that appear to be unusual but are not impossible. For example, a woman can weigh 500 pounds. Should her weight be declared an outlier or not? One solution to this dilemma is to ask whether or not this person would be considered as part of the target population for which you wish to make inferences. If the answer is yes, her weight probably should be included. Another alternative is to do the analysis both with and without the questionable outlier.

Transformations of Data

Variable transformation is one of the major operations in data processing. Transformations are often used to collapse categories of nominal or ordinal data to obtain a smaller, more usable number of categories. If running a univariate statistical program shows that some of the categories have been chosen by very few respondents, it may be sensible to combine them with similar categories. For nominal data, any categories conceivably could be combined, but for ordinal data, only adjacent categories should be combined. The decision to collapse categories is a compromise between having too many categories with some chosen by very few respondents and collapsing so much that information is lost.

Some statistical procedures are more easily performed with dichotomous, two-category, or 0,1 data. Categorical data with three or more categories are often transformed to a series of dummy variables with only two outcomes (0 or 1) for use in multivariate analyses (see Afifi & Clark, 1990).

Transformations are also used to change the units of interval data, to sum or otherwise combine variables to create a scale or other summary score, and to summarize skip patterns. In longitudinal data, it is often necessary to make transformations on data that are collected at different times. For example, "change" scores such as weight loss are often computed by subtracting data collected at time 1 from data collected at time 2.

We will first discuss types of transformations and then how to use them to obtain new variables. Finally, we will discuss the use of transformations to normalize data.

ARITHMETIC TRANSFORMATIONS

One of the simplest operations is the arithmetic transformation. Suppose gender has been coded male = 1 and female = 2 and you desire to use it as a 0,1 variable so that odds ratios (see Reynolds, 1977) can be computed. Subtracting a 1 from the variable will make the desired transformation. Height might be measured in centimeters and you want to report it in inches, so you divide the measurement by 2.54. Interaction predictor variables are often created by multiplying two predictor variables together, as illustrated in the previous section. To avoid errors, all such arithmetic transformations of the data should be done in the computer rather than by hand calculator prior to data entry. SPSS, BMDP, and SAS manuals provide specific instructions on how to perform such arithmetic operations.

The arithmetic operations commonly available are addition (+), subtraction (–), multiplication (*), division (/), and exponentiation (**) (raising a variable to a power—for example, squaring it). The statistical packages perform arithmetic operations in the reverse order from that in which you learned them—exponentiation first, then division and multiplication, and finally subtraction and addition. Parentheses can be used to control the order of operations, since quantities inside parentheses are evaluated first. For example, in the combination "(y+6)**.5," the computer first sums y and 6 and then computes the square root of the sum. If the parentheses were missing, the computer would first take the square root of 6 and then add it to y. For "avercost=(costa+costb)/2," again the computer will combine the quantity in the parentheses first and then divide by 2. If the parentheses were missing, the computer would divide "costb" by 2 and then add it to "costa."

FUNCTIONS OF DATA

In addition to the arithmetic operators, SPSS, SAS, and BMDP have numerous *functions* that can be used in data screening, transformations, and statistical analyses. Commonly used functions include taking the log of a variable, computing the mean of a variable, determining the maximum and minimum of a variable, assigning random numbers, recoding dates, and generating cumulative distribution functions of common distributions such as the normal. These functions can be used in combination with the arithmetic operations. For example, "z=log(y+100)" would result in a new variable called z being computed from the log of the sum of variable y plus 100.

COMPARISON OPERATORS

The major packages have functions called *comparison operators* that can be used in transformations or for case selection. For example, categories can be collapsed using comparison or logical operators embedded in *if-then* statements. Commonly used comparison operators include the following:

Symbols	Statement	Examples
gt, >	greater than	age > 18
ge, ≥	greater than or equal to	age ≥ 19
lt, <	less than	age < 66
le, ≤	less than or equal to	age ≤ 65
eq, =	equal	age = 19
ne, ≠	not equal to	age ≠ 18
and, &	both or all true	age > 18 and age < 66
or, I	either true	age < 18 or age > 65

These operators compare two or more variables, constants, or functions. The computer checks the truth of the statement containing the operator for each subject. For example, if the statement was (age greater than 18), the programs will check each subject's age to see if a number greater than 18 is given. If the statement was (age greater than 18 *and* age less than 66), it would be true only for persons 19-65 years of age. If the statement was (age less than 18 *or* age greater than 65), it would be true if the subject was either younger than 18 or older than 65.

The comparison operators are used in what are called *if-then* or *if-then else* statements. The form of an if-then statement is as follows: If (this statement is true) then (take this action). For example, you could write:

if (age>18) then (use this subject)
if (educat=1 or educat=2) then (recode neweduc to 1)

The if-then statements are used to select subjects, to transform variables already in the data set (often for use in tables), to create new variables that are added to the end of the data set, to make dummy variables, to replace missing values with imputed values (see Afifi & Clark, 1990), and to perform consistency checks on the data.

The form of writing the if-then statements varies by statistical package, but the result is essentially the same. The else clause is added to simplify entry of actions that have numerous possible outcomes. For example,

if (educat=1 or educat=2) then (educat=1) else (educat=2)

transforms the variable *educat* to a 1 if it originally was a 1 or 2, and to a 2 if it was anything else.

Skip Variables. Transformations must be used to create variables that are suitable for analysis from skip-and-fill questions (see Chapter 4). Often a single variable is created from a series of questions. For example, alcohol usage is often determined by first asking respondents if they drink. If they answer no, they skip a series of questions on what they drink and how much, and are coded zero. For those answering yes, their intake of each type of drink is multiplied by the amount of alcohol contained in that drink, and then the amounts are summed over the types of drinks to provide a single variable giving daily alcohol intake.

After performing the transformations to change the scale of a variable, to collapse variables, or to adjust for skips, it is important to check the results to see that the transformations were done correctly. Checking is sometimes done by choosing a few examples from the data set and doing them by hand to see if the results are the same as those the computer produced. A more comprehensive method for nominal and ordinal data is to compute a two-way table of the original variable against the transformed variable. The results in the interior of the table will show how the original and transformed results compare for all the cases. This is particularly useful when complex comparative statements are used.

TRANSFORMATIONS TO ACHIEVE NORMALITY

Transformations are commonly used to achieve approximate univariate *normality* out of a skewed or nonnormal distribution. Many tests of hypotheses and confidence limits are based on the assumption of a normal or Gaussian distribution. If data are normally distributed, their histogram should be symmetric and bell shaped. Because the normal distribution can be written as a mathematical expression, it is possible to use formal statistical tests to decide if data follow a normal distribution. These formal tests are sensitive to outliers, so it is important to screen the data first and remove obvious outliers.

A normal distribution is symmetric about its mean and median. The sample median is the middle observation if the sample size is odd or the average of two middle observations if it is even. It is approximately equal to the 50th percentile. Symmetry implies that the difference between the median (50th percentile) and, for example, the 25th percentile (P25) should be approximately equal to the difference between the 75th percentile (P75) and the median. Percentiles divide a sample into 100 equal parts; they can be produced by the SPSS FREQUEN-CIES, SAS UNIVARIATE, or BMDP 2D program.

Two commonly used graphical methods for determining whether a distribution is approximately normal are to plot a histogram and check whether it is symmetric, or to obtain a normal probability plot and check whether it follows a straight line. Histograms and normal probability plots can be obtained from SPSS, SAS, and BMDP programs.

There are also several formal tests for normality. The commonly used Shapiro-Wilks's *W* test is available in SPSS EXAMINE, SAS UNIVARIATE, and BMDP 2D. While good for small samples, this test can also be used on larger samples. For very large samples, the Kolmogorov-Smirnov D is often used. This is available in SPSS EXAMINE and SAS UNIVARIATE.

The skewness statistic indicates how nonsymmetric a distribution is. Skewness will be close to zero if a distribution is normal. If a distribution has a longer tail to the right, the skewness will be positive. If a distribution has a longer tail to the left, the skewness statistic will be negative. When the data are skewed, it is usually to the right. It is important to screen the data first for unusually large or small values, since outliers can have a large effect on the skewness statistic. SPSS and BMDP provide information on the standard error of the skewness statistic so the user can test if it is zero. A distribution that has a skewness greater than 0.8 is noticeably skewed.

If the skewness is significantly different from zero, you might want to consider transforming the data to reduce the skewness and obtain a closer approximation to a normal distribution, as discussed next.

There are several strategies to determine the appropriate transformation. If the theoretical distribution of the data is known, there may be a transformation that is known to transform the raw data toward normality. For example, the square-root transformation is commonly used for data that follow a Poisson distribution. When the researcher does not know the theoretical distribution that the data follow, power transformations should be considered (Hoaglin et al., 1983; Tukey, 1977).

Power Transformations. Power transformations take the form

$$(X + A)^P$$

where X signifies the variable, A is a constant (often zero), and P is the power that is used. For example, if $A = 0$ and $P = \frac{1}{2}$, then the transformation computes the square root of the data. Raising X to a power less than 1 reduces large values of X more than small values of X. As a result, it "draws in" the long right tail. As a simple example, suppose we had six observations with observed values of 1, 4, 9, 9, 16, and 25. The median is 9 and the mean is 10.67. The difference between the smallest value and the median is 8, but the difference between the largest value and the median is 16, which indicates a possible skewness to the right. Similarly, for the mean we would have $10.67 - 1 = 9.67$ and $25 - 10.67 = 14.33$. If we take the square root of each observation we obtain 1, 2, 3, 3, 4, and 5, which are symmetric about the mean or median.

Values of P less than 1 are chosen if the data are skewed to the right; values of P greater than 1 are chosen if the data are skewed to the left. When data are skewed to the right, progressively decreasing the value of P progressively reduces the skew to the right. As you decrease P, the distribution becomes approximately symmetric and finally skewed to the left. Common values of P that are tried are $\frac{1}{2}$, 0, and -1. Since taking the logarithm of the data is conceptually equivalent to $P = 0$ (Tukey, 1977), taking the log of the data transforms the distribution more than taking the square root. Similarly, taking the inverse of the data ($P = -1$) transforms it more than the log. When the inverse is taken, usually a negative sign is put in front of the result so that the direction of the numbers stays the same. When data are skewed to the left, the data are most often squared ($P = 2$).

The constant A can be used to improve the results once P is chosen. For example, if the data are skewed to the right and a log transformation (either natural or base 10) improves the results, but not quite enough, and the inverse transformation is too great, subtracting a constant will have the effect of decreasing the skewness. If all positive numbers are to be maintained, the constant must be less than the smallest value of X. An alternative to subtracting a constant A would be to try values of P between 0 (the log transformation) and -1, say, $-\frac{1}{2}$. Often the constant is used to avoid in-between values of P that are difficult to explain. Use of a constant is also thought by some investigators to shift the data to values with a more natural zero point. To decrease the effect of the transformation, add a positive constant A. (See Afifi & Clark, 1990, for a graphical method of choosing P and A developed by Hines & Hines, 1987.)

It should be kept in mind that a transformation that works well on your sample may not necessarily be the best transformation for the entire population. This is particularly true for small samples. For this reason, many investigators choose common transformations that have been used by others such as the log or square root, if these work reasonably well on their sample. Any of the methods mentioned previously to determine if the data are normal can be used to evaluate the results.

Advisability of Transformation to Normality. The decision on whether to transform is dependent on what statistical analyses you expect to use, the degree of nonnormality, and the variability of the data. Some statistical procedures, such as logistic regression, do not assume normality. Some statistical tests are quite robust to (i.e., unaffected by) lack of normality.

If the coefficient of variation (standard deviation divided by the mean) is less than one-third (see Hald, 1952) or the largest observation divided by the smallest is less than two (see Hoaglin et al., 1983) the data frequently are not sufficiently variable to make it worthwhile to perform a transformation. In addition, some types of distributions can never be transformed to approximate normality, although they may be brought closer. For example, a distribution with positive numbers where the mode (most common value) is at zero cannot be transposed to yield a normal distribution.

Once data are transformed, all inferences and discussions of the transformed variable must be made in terms of the newly transformed values. In deciding whether to use transformations, the reader must remember that some persons have difficulty understanding how transformations affect data. As a result, they may not understand inferences or discussions that depend on the transformations you have performed.

Other Kinds of Transformations. Other transformations sometimes are performed after statistical analysis is started. For example, in regression analysis, data are often transformed to achieve a straight line or plane; in analysis of variance, transformations are frequently used to reduce the interaction mean square. The power transformations can be used in making these transformations (see Tukey, 1977). There are particular techniques that are useful with particular statistical analyses. Our advice is to consult a textbook that discusses tests of normality for the analysis you wish to use, and examine the output available in the various computer programs to help you decide what transformations to use.

Transformations often make it possible to use standard statistical tests and confidence intervals for regression analysis, discriminant function analysis, analysis of variance, and so on, so that nonparametric methods or robust statistical techniques are not necessary.

Scale Evaluation

Different authors use the term *scale* somewhat differently. Babbie (1973) defines a scale as the assignment of scores to response patterns among several items making up a scale. He defines an index to be the summation of scores assigned to specific items according to the responses of the subjects. Thus, by his definition, a Guttman scale would be a scale, but a Likert summation of scores would be an index. Most other authors would define scaling as the process of assigning numbers to the measurement of attitude. By attitude, we mean the degree of positive or negative affect associated with some object or stimulus. Here we will use the word *scale* to apply to either indexes or scales.

LIKERT SCALES

The most commonly used scale procedure is the Likert scale, and the evaluation of already constructed Likert scales will be treated here. The construction of Likert scales is discussed in McKennell (1977), and an introduction to the fundamentals of unidimensional scaling theory and construction is given in McIver and Carmines (1981; see also DeVellis, 1991). Other possible measures of attitude include the Guttman scale (see Torgerson, 1958), Thurstone (see Edwards, 1957), and the semantic differential (see Osgood, Suci, & Tannenbaum, 1957). In using a Likert scale, one is scaling the subjects, but in Guttman and Thurstone scales, the procedure includes scaling both the stimuli and the subjects, separately.

Typical Likert scales consist of from 4 to 40 items. For example, an item might state, "I have trouble concentrating on tasks." Respondents typically are asked to state the extent to which they agree with each statement using a 5-point scale. For example, "strongly disagree" = 1, "disagree" = 2, "undecided" = 3, "agree" = 4, "strongly agree" = 5. Items that are worded negatively must have their scores reversed. For a 5-point scale, this is achieved by subtracting the original value from 6. This is done so that 5 always signifies strong agreement or approval. The scale score is typically obtained by summing the scores (including the reversed ones) for each item.

The use of a Likert scale has many advantages over attempting to gauge opinion with a single question. The answers to a single item have been shown to vary with format or wording to such an extent that we recommend forming multiple items into scales if the attitude being measured is an important part of the study. Examples of Likert scales can be obtained from the literature (e.g., Chun et al., 1975; George & Bearon, 1980; Kane & Kane, 1981; McDowell & Newell, 1987; Reeder et al., 1976; Robinson et al., 1973, 1991; Robinson & Shaver, 1973; Shaw & Wright, 1967).

Characteristics of a Good Likert Scale. The characteristics that we want to find in existing scales include parsimony, minimal overlap with other constructs under study, high validity and reliability, unidimensionality or known dimensionality, and summated scores that can be assumed to be interval or ratio data. The interest in minimal overlap with other constructs is an important facet of parsimony. The inclusion of numerous long and similar scales has been shown to be dysfunctional (see Andrews, 1984).

It is essential to understand and define clearly the attitude to be measured. Bollen (1989) points out that most researchers assume that subjects' attitudes "cause" their responses to items (and not vice versa). He therefore calls the items "effect indicators," as they reflect the effect of an attitude. Therefore, there must be evidence or a clear rationale for the selection of items for a Likert scale.

High validity and reliability (see Bollen, 1989; Carmines & Zeller, 1979) are essentials of a good scale. In this section, we briefly define validity and then discuss methods for measuring reliability. It is often possible to find information in the literature on the reliability of an existing scale you wish to use. Even when information is available from past studies, you should check the scale yourself, especially if your respondents differ from those on whom the scale was developed. Generally, reliability is more easily assessed, is more frequently assessed, and is assessed prior to assessing validity. Demonstration that a measure is reliable does not ensure that it is valid.

Validity. A scale is valid if it measures what it is supposed to measure. Validity can be assessed in any or all of three main ways: (a) by seeing whether the summated scale score predicts behavior that is assessed separately from the scale (criterion-related validity); (b) by assessing whether the items included cover the universe of content thought to be important (comprehensiveness of item coverage, content validity)—here knowledge of the attitude being measured is crucial; and (c) by determining whether it is correlated with other measures as expected from theoretical considerations (construct validity). Assessing validity by simply computing the correlation between the scale score and another criterion requires that both be measured accurately; otherwise, the evaluation of validity becomes quite subjective. You will need to use a scale with items that have clear and consistent meanings that represent the attitude you wish to measure. Additional measures of validity are presented by Bollen (1989).

Reliability. In this context, reliability is the degree to which the results are consistent across time (test-retest reliability), data collectors (stability), and items of the scale (homogeneity or internal consistency). Reliability is defined as the ratio of the variance of the true score to the variance of the actual measured score. It lies between zero and one. Carmines and Zeller (1979) recommend that scales ideally should have a reliability of at least 0.80; however, many widely used scales have reliabilities in the 0.65 to 0.80 range. In regression analysis, if the dependent variable has low reliability, the estimates of the slope coefficients and the mean of the dependent variable are not biased but the variability of the estimates is increased. If the independent or predictor variables have low reliability, the estimates of the slope coefficients are biased in a downward direction. The estimate of the variability of the dependent variable is not changed, but the variability of the estimates of independent variables is increased.

The methods usually used to assess reliability relate to one of two purposes. The first is to make sure that the reliability of the scale is sufficiently high. The second purpose is to determine the effects of each item on reliability. These two purposes become intertwined in that the reliability can sometimes be increased by removing items.

If it is possible to administer the scale twice to the same subjects, reliability can be assessed by obtaining the simple correlation of the *test-retest* summated scores. This would seem the simplest method, but it is often not feasible. In a typical survey, retesting is not done. When it can be performed, questions remain concerning when to do it. If you wait too long, the subjects could change their attitudes, but if you do it too soon, the subjects may remember and try to repeat what they did before.

The most commonly used reliability measure is called *Cronbach's alpha.* After the researcher has reversed the coding of items where needed, Cronbach's alpha can be calculated either from the original item values or from standardized item values. The scores for standardized items have a mean of zero and a variance of one. We denote the first calculation as "raw-data alpha" and the second as "standardized alpha." Raw-data alpha is computed using the variance-covariance matrix computed from the item values, where the diagonal of the matrix contains the variance of each item and the rest of the matrix is composed of the covariances between all pairs of items. The variance-covariance matrix of the standardized scores is the correlation matrix. The process of calculating the correlations standardizes the original item values. In either case, using the variance-covariance matrix or the correlation matrix, the formula for alpha is as follows:

$$\alpha = \frac{P}{P-1}\left(1 - \frac{\sum \text{diag}}{\sum \text{all entries}}\right)$$

where P equals the number of items, *diag* denotes the diagonal elements of the matrix, and *all entries* denotes all the elements of the matrix including the diagonal. Alpha can vary from 0 to 1. Alpha increases as the size of the off-diagonal elements (covariances or correlations) increases relative to the size of the diagonal elements (variances). Since standardized alpha is calculated from the correlation matrix, the variances in the diagonal are always 1s, so their sum is simply P or the number of items. Increasing the number of items (P) also increases alpha if the average magnitude of the covariances or correlations stays the same. This happens because, as P increases, the number of off-diagonal elements increases faster than the number of diagonal elements.

The decision as to whether to use the raw-data alpha or the standardized alpha is complicated. Most researchers use summated scale scores computed from the raw data. As we mentioned in the section on transformations, when transformations are made on data inferences can be made only to the transformed data. In the case of Cronbach's alpha, when the standardized alpha is used inferences can be assumed to apply only to the standardized items; inferences cannot automatically be assumed to apply to the raw data for the population of persons from whom the sample of subjects was drawn. If it can be assumed that the population variances of the raw-data items are equal, then it can be assumed that standardizing the items makes no difference and that the results obtained with the standardized alpha also apply to the raw-data scale. If it *cannot* be assumed that the items have equal variances in the underlying population, then the raw data alpha should be used if raw-data scores are summed.

The researcher can use two procedures when attempting to test the validity of the above assumptions. First, he or she can examine the actual range and variances of the raw item scores in the sample. If it can be concluded that they are equivalent across items, it strengthens the researcher's confidence that the standardized alpha can be used. Second, the researcher can compare the standardized alpha to the raw-data alpha. The size of the two alphas will be similar if the sample variances are similar, but can be quite different if the sample variances are substantially unequal.

Alpha is equal to either reliability or a lower bound to reliability, depending upon the assumptions made. It provides a conservative measure of the true reliability. See Bollen (1989) for an informative summary of the assumptions made in the above measures of reliability.

Alpha can be computed from a covariance or correlation matrix output of a computer program, but the easiest way to obtain it is to use the RELIABILITY program in SPSS. This program will provide the overall standardized or raw-data alpha for your scale as well as numerous other useful statistics. It will also help you decide how to remove items from a scale if this is desired. Usually, well-known scales are used untouched, for comparability and other reasons. If, however, you desire to remove some items, one strategy for deciding which ones to remove is to examine the reliability of the scale with the candidate item removed. If the alpha goes up or stays the same, that item is a candidate for removal. The RELIABILITY program provides the value of alpha if each item and only that item is deleted from the scale. It also provides the correlation of each item with the corrected total score (that item removed) as well as other useful statistics. Each item should be positively and appreciably correlated with the corrected total score. If it is not, this may indicate that an item either does not improve reliability of the scale or measures something different from the majority of the items. An item that does not contribute to reliability or that pertains to a different attitude can be removed and the program rerun to search for additional candidate items.

Additional Evaluation Techniques. Another technique is to use the *conditional statements* to select subjects that score in the top 25% and bottom 25% on total score and to compute the average score for each item for both of these subgroups. An item that does not have a high average for the top 25% subjects or a low average for the bottom 25% of the subjects is not behaving consistently and could be considered a candidate for removal. Items can also be considered for removal if they have an appreciably smaller standard deviation than others in the scale, since this probably indicates that most respondents are heaping in only one or two categories.

It is also possible to divide the sample into subgroups based on gender or age. For research purposes, suppose that you would like the scale to be used in a similar fashion by males and females or young and old persons. It is not that you expect the same mean for males and females for each item, but that you prefer they use a similar frame of reference. The standard deviations and correlations of the items can be examined for each subgroup. You may be more interested in items that have a sizable standard deviation (not everyone answers the same) for each subgroup and similar simple correlations within each group. The RELI-ABILITY program can also be run on subgroups to gain further insight into the reliability of the scale.

Number of Dimensions. One concern that researchers have with Likert scales is uncertainty about their unidimensionality. Suppose half the items in a scale contribute to one dimension and the other half to another independent dimension. From the tests given previously, a researcher might miss the presence of the two dimensions, and certainly will not know what items belong to which dimension. Obviously, scales that measure along a single dimension are simpler to interpret. It may be, however, that overlapping dimensions are needed to measure the complexity of the attitude structure. See McKennell (1977) for further discussion of this and methods for deciphering the dimensions.

Several empirical methods are useful in deciding if several dimensions exist. One is simply to read the items and try to decide if they all fall along a single dimension. The second is to obtain the simple correlation matrix and examine it to see if two or more clusters of items exist that are highly intercorrelated within each cluster but uncorrelated or negatively correlated between clusters. The problem with the second approach is that while it is relatively simple to see the separate sets after the items have been ordered so that those within each cluster (or factor) are adjacent, it is very difficult to see when the items are all mixed up.

To deal with the problems described above, two statistical techniques, cluster analysis and factor analysis, have been recommended (see McKennell, 1977). These help to determine whether separate dimensions exist and what items belong to which dimension. If cluster analysis is used, you will want to run a program that clusters the *variables* and not the subjects, since it is the items that are being examined. The VARCLUS procedure in SAS and the 1M program in BMDP are suitable.

Factor analysis is more widely known and used (see Kim & Mueller, 1978, for an introduction to factor analysis). If the scale is strictly one-dimensional, you would expect to see a single principal component or factor explain a sizable proportion of the variance. If overlapping dimensions are present, several factors may emerge. We recommend the use of an oblique rotation, so that the separate factors are not forced to be uncorrelated, and factor scores be saved. The larger factor loadings will show which items contribute most to which factor. If the factors obtained (using an oblique rotation) are clearly uncorrelated and the items load on separate factors, the possibility of different dimensions should be explored. A scree plot can be used to decide upon the number of factors to consider. A second factor analysis of the factor scores can be performed to see if a single factor results (see Clark, Aneshensel, Frerichs, & Morgan, 1981, for an example of such an analysis). If a single factor is obtained, there is a basis to argue for an overall dimension composed of overlapping dimensions. SPSS, SAS, and BMDP will perform oblique rotations of the factors.

If one has an a priori hypothesis regarding the number of dimensions that underlie a scale, confirmatory factor analysis should be considered (see Long, 1983, for an explanation of the uses of confirmatory factor analysis).

Weighting Items. Another concern about using Likert scales is whether the items should be summed directly or differentially weighted prior to summing. Following Likert, most existing scales were developed and tested as undifferentiated sums of the items. It is simpler to make comparisons with past results if the items are treated the same way. Some researchers feel uneasy about this if a factor analysis of the items shows that the factor score coefficients (or factor loadings) are quite unequal; they may desire to use a differentially weighted sum or a factor score. If the factor analysis provides clear and understandable factors, use of the factor scores may be desirable. However, typically a high correlation will be obtained between summated and factor scores so that the simpler summated scores are preferred. One empirical approach is to do it both ways (summing the items and computing separate factor scores) and see which result is most useful in subsequent analyses.

Imputation of Missing Values in Likert Scales. It should be noted that methods of imputing missing values can also apply to Likert scales. Often a respondent will fail to answer only one or two items in a Likert scale with numerous items. There are several methods used to impute item scores. Some investigators will assign the average score for that item from those who did answer the item. Mean substitution is easily implemented in SPSS. Others treat it as an "undecided" and, for example, will assign a score of 3 on a 5-point scale. Some assign a score that reflects the subject's answers on other items. For example, suppose there were 6 items but a subject answered only 5, with a total score of 20. The subject's average score is 20/5 = 4; that average can be assigned to the missing item so the subject's summated score is 20 + 4 = 24. A more complex method is to perform a regression analysis predicting the missing item from other items, using values from subjects who answered all the items. Then, this regression equation is used to estimate the missing item using the method given in the section on missing values. If a respondent is missing most of the items, most investigators would declare the summated score to be missing. If one or more items have excessive missing values, the items should be examined for problems and possibly excluded.

Summary of Likert Scales. In checking Likert scales, usually a variety of methods are used until a consensus can be reached on how respondents are using the scale. The results from the cluster analysis should agree to a reasonable extent with the factor analysis. The items that cluster will likely load on the same factor. If time is limited and you are sure that the scale is unidimensional, use of the RELIABILITY program in SPSS may be all that is needed.

All scales are compromises. If your only concern is obtaining high reliability, this can be accomplished by making minor wording changes in the items during scale development until you obtain high between-item correlations. This, however, usually results in low validity. Conversely, developing a variety of items that covers the full range of content may lower the scale's reliability and result in multiple overlapping dimensions rather than a single dimension, though it may also lead to a scale with high validity.

In performing the previously mentioned checks on Likert scales, an interval scale is assumed both at the item level and in the summated scale that is created. Most of the statistics used (means, covariances, and correlations) require an interval scale. Although considerable discussion is given in Sonquist and Dunkelberg (1977) concerning the reasonableness of the summated score being an interval scale, at the item level, it is an assumption that is commonly made in order to use available statistics.

Creation of Subfiles for Analysis

When large data sets exist, subfiles often are created for particular analyses. For example, in surveys it is not unusual to end up with 600 to 1,000 variables. For a given research task, an investigator may wish to use only 15 variables. In order to save computer time it is useful to create a *subfile* with only the desired variables. Also, if numerous investigators are using the same data set and some are not closely connected with the project, it is often prudent to give each investigator an agreed-upon subset of the data rather than the entire data set. If errors are found in any of the subfiles, corrections must be made in the master file.

Investigators often create a *subfile of cases* when they have a very large sample size, and run though their proposed analyses on the smaller sample as a way of screening out obviously useless statistical analyses. The statements needed to run the statistical packages can also be edited and corrected using the smaller sample size. This saves computer time. For example, in a study of 45,000 birth certificates it makes sense to run preliminary analyses on a subsample. The three package programs have procedures for creating subfiles of variables or cases. In addition, the use of subfiles that are random samples of the total files can be useful for cross-validating results. SPSS, SAS, and BMDP provide options for taking random samples of the cases.

With cleaned, transformed, and documented working files, the investigators are finally ready to perform the needed statistical analyses and write their reports and articles.

6. A CHECKLIST FOR STUDY DOCUMENTATION

Documentation is a continuing process that starts at the conception of the study and provides an audit trail for all steps (and missteps) along the way. In earlier chapters we have stressed the crucial importance of good records and notes. Here we offer an annotated checklist of key points that should be documented. Data storage, disposal of collection forms, and placing the data in the public domain are briefly discussed.

Sample Design

Describe the population sampled, the method of sampling, sampling procedures and problems, and the final sample. If strata or clusters were taken, they also should be described. Record the names and characteristics of any sample-weighting variables used.

Data Collection Instrument

Keep copies of all data collection instruments that were used. Any nonobvious rationale for the inclusion of a variable should be noted. Document the origin and authorship of all materials adopted or adapted from the work of other researchers. Keep an annotated copy of the final instruments. Pretests and pilot tests should be described, together with summaries of the changes they inspired.

Data Collection Training and Procedures

Include instruction and training materials prepared for interviewers or data abstractors. Important topics include the objectives, funding, and sponsorship of the study, provisions for confidentiality, anticipated problems or questions the workers may face, and procedures for quality control.

Coding of Data

Document carefully and explicitly all codes assigned to data gathered from interviews, records, observations, and so on. For precoded data collection instruments an annotated copy of the instrument is valuable, but may lack some needed information. Before the use of the newer data entry systems, codebooks were written that included each variable's number, name, location, format (written in fixed-format notation, such as F3.1), and information about how data were coded. Now, the needed portion of codebooks comes from the data entry program as described below. In addition, either references or reasons for coding decisions may need to be kept. Special problems should be noted.

Data Entry for Computerized Files

At minimum, the documentation must describe fully the variables that are included in the data set. The description might include names, the correspondence between the computerized data codes and the original data items, and the formats and statistical program linkages of the computer-stored data files. Without this documentation, a raw-data file is useless because there is no "key" to explain the location of data or the meaning of the data included in the file. Information should be kept about both the cleaning status of the data and the process by which data were cleaned. Include information about the range of acceptable values for each variable and the kinds of consistency checks that have been made between variables.

Data entry programs developed for the major statistical analysis packages now provide much of this information in computer-readable form as a by-product of the data file definition and data entry actions. Printouts of this information, suitably annotated by hand or with a word-processing program, can serve as excellent documentation.

Data Processing That Precedes Analysis

Document how missing values and outliers are handled, and keep a record of what transformations are used and how scales are checked. These actions modify the field-collected data in ways that facilitate statistical analysis and influence research conclusions. The actions taken, the problems they serve to correct, and any underlying assumptions must be documented in detail, and the order of execution noted. Annotated statistical program instructions provide an efficient way to do this.

Frequency Distributions for All Study Variables

These are sometimes referred to as "master frequencies." A copy should be available to all users of the data set.

Archives of Data Files

Archive copies of the data should be transferred to removable media (magnetic tape, floppy diskettes, removable hard-disk cartridges, or the like) for safekeeping away from the computer system. Multiple backups are recommended, since tapes and disks can either be defective or become defective over time. It is prudent, also, to create a more general form of the file for safekeeping. This maximizes one's ability to transfer the data and subsequent analyses to other computer hardware systems or to another statistical package. If the original data entry produces a raw-data file to which variable labels, definitions, and so on subsequently are added using one of the statistical packages, both the raw data and the additional information should be stored in computer-readable form.

Researchers often keep hard copies of raw-data files (if the data set is not too large), with verbatim answers to any uncoded, open-ended questions, keyed to the respondents' identification numbers.

After Data Processing and Analysis Are Finished

DISPOSAL OF DATA COLLECTION FORMS

A policy should be established and executed for disposal of original field data. The creation of full and timely documentation allows data collection forms to be destroyed. We prefer shredding of data collection forms rather than storing them for three reasons: (a) Storage can require large amounts of space, (b) preserving the confidentiality of stored documents is difficult, and (c) the certainty that the original documents will be destroyed creates an incentive for timely and complete data entry and cleaning.

Proper and timely destruction of data collection forms is particularly important when data are collected that reveal either illegal or potentially embarrassing behavior on the part of respondents. In even the most secure locations and even when researchers think all possible identifying information has been stripped from the data set, confidentiality protection for study data is not absolute, since access often can be obtained through subpoena. Proper and timely destruction of data forms reduces this risk.

MOVING DATA INTO PUBLIC DOMAIN

As Sieber (1991) notes, while "openness is a familiar idea in scientific research, . . . until recently, openness in science has meant publishing one's methods and results" (p. 1). The norms are beginning to change in this regard. Issues such as the high cost of original data collection, widely publicized incidents of research fraud, improved technology for storing and inexpensively distributing large data sets, and increased recognition that it is important to replicate analyses, particularly when findings are new or controversial, are contributing to increased data sharing.

The National Academy of Sciences, many professional associations, major funding agencies, journals, and universities are now encouraging, recommending, or requiring that researchers make raw data available to others. No single policy has been established, so groups differ in the specifics of their recommendations, but all provide exceptions or mandate protection for data sets in which individuals can be identified. When data are collected under federal contract, "the Contractor grants to the Government . . . a paid-up, non-exclusive, irrevocable worldwide license in such copyrighted data to reproduce, prepare derivative works, distribute copies to the public, and perform publicly and display publicly by or on behalf of the Government" (Commerce Clearing House, 1991). The National Science Foundation (1989) explicitly requires that data collected under grants be made available to other researchers "at no more than incremental cost and within a reasonable time," while the Public Health Service requires that data be made available to the federal government (U.S. Department of Health and Human Services, 1990). The *American Journal of Public Health* (1991) requires that authors retain data for at least three years and make it available to the editor on request. Many professional associations have developed policies regarding the form and timely dissemination of research findings and data sets and the protection of human subjects within research settings. Often these have been incorporated in formal codes of ethics (e.g., American Sociological Association, 1988) or supervised by standing committees of the professional association such as the American Psychological Association's Committee on Standards in Research (e.g., Grisso et al., 1991).

While some data sets are shared through informal networks, data increasingly are being placed in archives such as those run by the Institute for Social Science Research at UCLA and the Interuniversity Consortium for Political and Social Research (ICPSR). The process of placing data in a publicly accessible archive raises "increasingly complex questions concerning . . . data ownership, authorship, the responsibility for sharing data, balancing the rights of academic freedom versus the need for informed supervision, and determining the timing and method for releasing 'sensitive' results to the public" (Grisso et al., 1991). Nonetheless, we recommend that data sets be moved into archives as soon as they have been cleaned and documented, and preliminary analyses have been completed. Sometimes it is appropriate to ask that data sets be archived with restricted access for some period of time following the completion of data collection, but we feel that such restricted access should not exceed five years. When a data set is moved to archives, the researcher must be sure that full documentation accompanies the data set and that all identifying information is stripped from it. Groups such as ICPSR have protocols to assist the researcher in ensuring that data are archived appropriately (see Geda, 1991; Stephenson, n.d.). For more information on the history and current status of data sharing in the social sciences, we recommend Sieber (1991).

REFERENCES

ADAMS, R. N., and PREISS, J. J. (1960) Human Organization Research: Field Relations and Techniques. Homewood, IL: Dorsey.

ADAY, L. A. (1989) Designing and Conducting Health Surveys: A Comprehensive Guide. San Francisco: Jossey-Bass.

AFIFI, A. A., and CLARK, V. (1990) Computer-Aided Multivariate Analysis (2nd ed.). New York: Van Nostrand Reinhold.

ALWIN, D. F. (ed.) (1991, August) Research on Survey Quality. Special issue of Sociological Methods and Research, Volume 20.

American Journal of Public Health (1991) "Information for authors." Vol. 81: 134-138.

American Sociological Association (1988) "Code of ethics." December 2.

ANDERSON, A. B., BASILEVSKY, A., and HUM, D. P. J. (1983) "Missing data: A review of the literature," pp. 415-494 in P. H. Rossi, J. D. Wright, and A. B. Anderson (eds.) Handbook of Survey Research. New York: Academic Press.

ANDERSON, B. A., SILVER, B. D., and ABRAMSON, P. R. (1988a) "The effects of race of the interviewer on measures of electoral participation by blacks in SRC national election studies." Public Opinion Quarterly 52: 53-83.

ANDERSON, B. A., SILVER, B. D., and ABRAMSON, P. R. (1988b) "The effects of the race of the interviewer on race-related attitudes of black respondents in SRC/CPS national election studies." Public Opinion Quarterly 52: 289-324.

ANDREWS, F. (1984) "Construct validity and error components of survey measures: A structural modeling approach." Public Opinion Quarterly 48(2): 409-442.

BABBIE, E. R. (1973) Survey Research Methods. Belmont, CA: Wadsworth.

BAILEY, K. D. (1987) Methods of Social Research (3rd ed.). New York: Free Press.

BARNETT, V., and LEWIS, T. (1984) Outliers in Statistical Data (2nd ed.). New York: John Wiley.

BOLLEN, K. A. (1989) Structural Equations With Latent Variables. New York: John Wiley.

BOONE, M. S., and WOOD, J. T. (1992) Computer Applications for Anthropologists. Belmont, CA: Wadsworth.

BRADBURN, N. M. (1983) "Response effects," pp. 289-328 in P. H. Rossi, J. D. Wright, and A. B. Anderson (eds.) Handbook of Survey Research. New York: Academic Press.

BRADBURN, N. M., SUDMAN, S., and Associates (1979) Improving Interview Method and Questionnaire Design. San Francisco: Jossey-Bass.

BREWER, J., and HUNTER, A. (1989) Multimethod Research: A Synthesis of Styles. Newbury Park, CA: Sage.

CAMPBELL, B. (1981) "Race of interviewer effects among southern adolescents." Public Opinion Quarterly 45: 231-244.

CARMINES, E. G., and ZELLER, R. A. (1979) Reliability and Validity Assessment. Beverly Hills, CA: Sage.

CHATTERJEE, S., and HADI, A. S. (1988) Sensitivity Analysis in Linear Regression. New York: John Wiley.

CHUN, K. T., COBB, S., and FRENCH, J. R. P., Jr. (1975) Measures for Psychological Assessment: A Guide to 3,000 Original Sources and Their Applications. Ann Arbor: University of Michigan, Institute for Social Research, Survey Research Center.

CLARK, V. A., ANESHENSEL, C., FRERICHS, R., and MORGAN, T. (1981) "Analysis of effects of sex and age in response to items on the CES-D Scale." Psychiatry Research 5: 171-181.

Commerce Clearing House, Inc. (1991) Federal Acquisition Regulation (FAR), Subchapter A—General, Part 1, Federal Acquisition Regulations System. Chicago, IL: Commerce Clearing House.

CONVERSE, J. M., and PRESSER, S. (1986) Survey Questions: Handcrafting the Standardized Questionnaire. Sage University Paper series on Quantitative Applications in the Social Sciences, 07-063. Beverly Hills, CA: Sage.

CONVERSE, P. E. (1970). "Attitudes and non-attitudes: Continuation of a dialogue," pp. 168-189 in E. R. Tulte (ed.) The Quantitative Analysis of Social Problems. Menlo Park, CA: Addison-Wesley.

COOK, R. D., and WEISBERG, S. (1982) Residuals and Influence in Regression. New York: Chapman & Hall.

COTTER, P. R., COHEN, J., and COULTER, P. B. (1982) "Race-of-interviewer effects in telephone interviews." Public Opinion Quarterly 46: 278-284.

DAVID, M., LITTLE, R. J. A., SAMUHEL, M. E., and TRIEST, R. K. (1986) "Alternative methods for CPS income imputation." Journal of the American Statistical Association 81(393): 29-41.

DEROGATIS, L. R., and SPENCER, P. M. (1982) The Brief Symptom Inventory (BSI). Riderwood, MD: Clinical Psychometric Research.

DEVELLIS, R. F. (1991) Scale Development: Theory and Application. Applied Social Research Methods, Volume 26. Newbury Park, CA: Sage.

DILLMAN, D. A. (1978) Mail and Telephone Surveys: The Total Design Method. New York: John Wiley.

DUNCAN, O. D., and STENBECK, M. (1988) "No opinion or not sure?" Public Opinion Quarterly 52: 513-525.

DUNN, O. J., and CLARK, V. A. (1987) Applied Statistics: Analysis of Variance and Regression (2nd ed.). New York: John Wiley.

EDWARDS, A. L. (1957) Techniques of Attitude Scale Construction. New York: Appleton-Century-Crofts.

FAULKENBERRY, G. D., and MASON, R. (1978) "Characteristics of nonopinion and no opinion response groups." Public Opinion Quarterly 42: 533-543.

FIECK, L. F. (1989) "Latent class analysis of survey questions that include 'Don't Know' responses." Public Opinion Quarterly 53: 525-547.

FINK, A., and KOSECOFF, J. (1985) How to Conduct Surveys: A Step-by-Step Guide. Beverly Hills, CA: Sage.

FLEISS, J. L. (1981) Statistical Methods for Rates and Proportions (2nd ed.). New York: John Wiley.

FLEISS, J. L. (1986) The Design and Analysis of Clinical Experiments. New York: John Wiley.

FORD, B. L. (1983) "An overview of hot-deck procedures in incomplete data," pp. 185-207 in W. G. Madow, I. Olken, and D. B. Rubin (eds.) Sample Surveys, Vol. 2: Theory and Bibliographies. New York: Academic Press.

FREY, J. H. (1989) Survey Research by Telephone (2nd ed.). Newbury Park, CA: Sage.

GEDA, C. L. (1991) "The Inter-University Consortium for Political and Social Research." American Economic Association Newsletter (March): 16-18.

GEORGE, L. K., and BEARON, L. B. (1980) Quality of Life in Older Persons. New York: Human Sciences Press.

GRISSO, T., BALDWIN, E., BLANCK, P. D., ROTHERAM-BORUS, M. J., SCHOOLER, N. R., and THOMPSON, T. (1991) "Standards in research: APA's mechanism for monitoring the challenges." American Psychologist 46: 758-766.

HALD, A. (1952) Statistical Theory With Engineering Applications. New York: John Wiley.

HALL, E. T. (1966) The Hidden Dimension. Garden City, NY: Doubleday.

HINES, W. G., and HINES, R. J. O. (1987) "Quick graphical power: Hyphen transformation selection." American Statistician 41: 21-24.

HOAGLIN, D. C., MOSTELLER, F., and TUKEY, J. W. (eds.) (1983) Understanding Robust and Exploratory Data Analysis. New York: John Wiley.

HOSMER, D. W., and LEMESHOW, S. (1989) Applied Logistic Regression. New York: John Wiley.

HYMAN, H. H. (1972) Secondary Analysis of Sample Surveys: Principles, Procedures, and Potentialities. New York: John Wiley.

JOBE, J. B., and LOFTUS, E. F. (eds.) (1991) Cognition and Survey Measurement. Special issue of Applied Cognitive Psychology, Volume 5.

KALTON, G., and KASPRZYK, D. (1986) "The treatment of missing survey data." Survey Methodology 12(1): 1-16.

KANE, R. A., and KANE, R. L. (1981) Assessing the Elderly: A Practical Guide to Measurement. Lexington, MA: Lexington.

KEANE, T. M., CADDELL, J. M., and TAYLOR, K. L. (1988) "Mississippi Scale for combat-related posttraumatic stress disorder: Three studies in reliability and validity." Journal of Consulting and Clinical Psychology 56(1): 85-90.

KIECOLT, K. J., and NATHAN, L. E. (1985) Secondary Analysis of Survey Data. Sage University Paper series on Quantitative Applications in the Social Sciences, 07-053. Beverly Hills, CA: Sage.

KIM, J. O., and MUELLER, C. W. (1978) Introduction to Factor Analysis. Sage University Paper series on Quantitative Applications in the Social Sciences, 07-013. Beverly Hills, CA: Sage.

KISH, L. (1965) Survey Sampling. New York: John Wiley.

LITTLE, R. J. A., and RUBIN, D. B. (1987) Statistical Analysis With Missing Data. New York: John Wiley.

LITTLE, R. J. A., and RUBIN, D. B. (1990) "The analysis of social science data with missing values," pp. 374-409 in J. Fox and J. S. Long (eds.) Modern Methods of Data Analysis. Newbury Park, CA: Sage.

LONG, J. S. (1983) Confirmatory Factor Analysis. Sage University Paper series on Quantitative Applications in the Social Sciences, 07-033. Beverly Hills, CA: Sage.

McDOWELL, I., and NEWELL, C. (1987) Measuring Health: A Guide to Rating Scales and Questionnaires. New York: Oxford University Press.

McIVER, J. P., and CARMINES, E. G. (1981) Unidimensional Scaling. Sage University Paper series on Quantitative Applications in the Social Sciences, 07-024. Beverly Hills, CA: Sage.

McKENNELL, A. C. (1977) "Attitude scale construction," pp. 183-220 in C. A. O'Muircheataugh and C. Payne (eds.) Exploring Data Structures, Vol. 1: The Analysis of Survey Data. New York: John Wiley.

MILES, M. B., and HUBERMAN, A. M. (1984) Qualitative Data Analysis: A Sourcebook of New Methods. Beverly Hills, CA: Sage.

National Science Foundation (1989) Notice 106 (April 17). Washington, DC: Government Printing Office.

OSGOOD, C. E., SUCI, G. J., and TANNENBAUM, P. H. (1957) The Measurement of Meaning. Urbana: University of Illinois Press.

PATTON, M. Q. (1990) Qualitative Evaluation and Research Methods. London: Sage.

POE, G. S., SEEMAN, I., McLAUGHLIN, J., MEHL, E., and DIETZ, M. (1988) "'Don't Know' boxes in factual questions in a mail questionnaire: Effects on level and quality of response." Public Opinion Quarterly 52: 212-222.

POOR, A. (1990) The Data Exchange. Homewood, IL: Dow Jones-Irwin.

PRESSER, H., and SCHUMAN, H. (1989) "The measurement of the middle position in attitude surveys," pp. 108-123 in E. Singer and S. Presser (eds.) Survey Research Methods: A Reader. Chicago: University of Chicago Press.

REEDER, L. G., RAMACHER, L., and GORELNIK, S. (1976) Handbook of Scales and Indices of Health Behavior. Pacific Palisades, CA: Goodyear.

REESE, S. D., DANIELSON, W. A., SHOEMAKER, P. J., CHANG, T. K., and HSU, H. L. (1986) "Ethnicity-of-interviewer effects among Mexican-Americans and Anglos." Public Opinion Quarterly 50: 563-572.

REYNOLDS, H. T. (1977) Analysis of Nominal Data. Sage University Paper series on Quantitative Applications in the Social Sciences, 07-007. Beverly Hills, CA: Sage.

ROBINSON, J. P., RUSK, J. G., and HEAD, K. B. (1973) Measures of Political Attitudes. Ann Arbor: University of Michigan, Institute for Social Research.

ROBINSON, J. P., and SHAVER, P. R. (1973) Measures of Social Psychological Attitudes. Ann Arbor: University of Michigan, Institute for Social Research, Survey Research Center.

ROBINSON, J. P., SHAVER, P. R., and WRIGHTSMAN, L. S. (1991) Measures of Personality and Social Psychological Attitudes. New York: Academic Press.

ROUSSEEUW, P. J., and VAN ZOMEREN, B. C. (1990) "Unmasking multivariate outliers and leverage points." Journal of the American Statistical Association 85: 633-639.

SCHUMAN, H., and CONVERSE, J. M. (1989) "The effects of black and white interviewers on black responses," pp. 247-271 in E. Singer and S. Presser (eds.) Survey Research Methods: A Reader. Chicago: University of Chicago Press.

SCRIMSHAW, S. C. M., and HURTADO, E. (1987) Rapid Assessment Procedures for Nutrition and Primary Health Care. Los Angeles: University of California, Latin American Center Publications.

SHAW, M. E., and WRIGHT, J. M. (1967) Scales for the Measurement of Attitudes. New York: McGraw-Hill.

SHEATSLEY, P. B. (1983) "Questionnaire construction and item writing," pp. 195-230 in P. H. Rossi, J. D. Wright, and A. B. Anderson (eds.) Handbook of Survey Research. New York: Academic Press.

SIEBER, J. E. (ed.) (1991) Sharing Social Science Data. Newbury Park, CA: Sage.

SINGER, E., FRANKEL, M. R., and GLASSMAN, M. B. (1989) "The effect of interviewer characteristics and expectations on response," pp. 272-287 in E. Singer and S.

Presser (eds.) Survey Research Methods: A Reader. Chicago: University of Chicago Press.

SONQUIST, J. A., and DUNKELBERG, W. C. (1977) Survey and Opinion Research: Procedures for Processing and Analysis. Englewood Cliffs, NJ: Prentice-Hall.

SPRADLEY, J. P. (1980) Participant Observation. New York: Holt, Rinehart & Winston.

STEPHENSON, E. (n.d.) Retention and Archiving of Survey Material. Los Angeles: University of California, Institute for Social Science Research.

STEWART, D. W., and KAMINS, M. A. (1993) Secondary Research: Information Sources and Methods. Applied Social Research Methods, Volume 4. Thousand Oaks, CA: Sage.

SUDMAN, S., and BRADBURN, N. M. (1982) Asking Questions. San Francisco: Jossey-Bass.

Survey Research Center (1976) Interviewer's Manual (rev. ed.). Ann Arbor: University of Michigan, Institute for Social Research, Survey Research Center.

TORGERSON, W. S. (1958) Theory and Methods of Scaling. New York: John Wiley.

TUKEY, J. W. (1977) Exploratory Data Analysis. Reading, MA: Addison-Wesley.

TURNER, R., NIGG, J. M., and HELLER PAZ, D. (1986) Waiting for Disaster: Earthquake Watch in Southern California. Berkeley: University of California Press.

U.S. Bureau of the Census (1970) 1970 Census, Industry and Occupation Coding Training Manual. Washington, DC: Government Printing Office.

U.S. Bureau of the Census (1992) 1990 Census of Population: Alphabetical Index of Industries and Occupations. Washington, DC: Government Printing Office.

U.S. Department of Health and Human Services. (1990) Public Health Service, PHS Grants Policy Statement. DHHS Publication (OASH) 90-50,000 (rev.). October 1. Washington, DC: Government Printing Office.

U.S. Office of Management and Budget (1990) Data Editing in Federal Statistical Agencies. Prepared by Subcommittee on Data Editing in Federal Statistical Agencies, Federal Committee on Statistical Methodology, Statistical Policy Office, Office of Information and Regulatory Affairs, Office of Management and Budget. Washington, DC: Government Printing Office.

VAN DUSEN, R. A., and ZILL, N. (eds.) (1975) Basic Background Items for U.S. Household Surveys. Washington, DC: Social Science Research Council, Center for Coordination of Research on Social Indicators.

WEBB, E. J., CAMPBELL, D. T., SCHWARTZ, R. D., and SUCHREST, L. (1966) Unobtrusive Measures: Nonreactive Research in the Social Sciences. Chicago: Rand McNally.

WEBER, R. P. (1985) Basic Content Analysis. Sage University Paper series on Quantitative Applications in the Social Sciences, 07-049. Beverly Hills, CA: Sage.

WEEKS, M. F., and MOORE, R. P. (1981) "Ethnicity-of-interviewer effects on ethnic respondents." Public Opinion Quarterly 45: 245-249.

WEINBERG, E. (1983) "Data collection: Planning and management," pp. 329-358 in P. H. Rossi, J. D. Wright, and A. B. Anderson (eds.) Handbook of Survey Research. New York: Academic Press.

RELEVANT SOFTWARE MANUALS

BMDP Data Entry (1991).

BMDP Statistical Software Manual, Vol. 1, for 1990 Software Release (see Chapter 2, "Data").

88

DBMS/COPY.
SAS IBM 370 Formats and Informats.
SAS/FSP Guide, Version 6 (1987) (data entry).
SAS Procedures Guide, Release 6.03 (1988).
SAS Language Guide for Personal Computers, Version 6 (1987).
SPSS Data Entry II for the IBM PC/XT/AT and PS/2 (1987).
SPSS/PC+ V2.0 Base Manual (1988), by Marija J. Norusis. Chicago: SPSS Inc.
SPSS/PC+ Update for V3.0 and V3.1 (1989).

ABOUT THE AUTHORS

LINDA B. BOURQUE is Professor and Head of the Division of Population and Family Health, and Vice Chair of the Department of Community Health Sciences, in the School of Public Health at the University of California at Los Angeles, where she teaches courses in research design and survey methodology. Her research is in the area of intentional and unintentional injury. She is the author or coauthor of 40 scientific articles and the book *Defining Rape*. She received her Ph.D. in sociology from Duke University.

VIRGINIA A. CLARK is Professor Emeritus of Biostatistics in the School of Public Health and Biomathematics in the School of Medicine at the University of California at Los Angeles. She is an expert in multivariate analysis and has consulted in biomedical and economic studies. She is author of more than 80 scientific articles and coauthor of four textbooks: *Preparation for Basic Statistics* (with Michael E. Tarter), *Applied Statistics: Analysis of Variance and Regression* (2nd ed.) (with O. Jean Dunn), *Survival Distributions: Reliability Applications in the Biomedical Sciences* (with Alan Gross), and *Computer-Aided Multivariate Analysis* (2nd ed.) (with A. A. Afifi). She received her Ph.D. in biostatistics from the University of California at Los Angeles.